The South Slavs in Utah: A Social History

Joseph Stipanovich

THE SOUTH SLAVS IN UTAH:

A Social History

By

Joseph Stipanovich

Printed in 1975 by

R AND E RESEARCH ASSOCIATES
4843 Mission Street, San Francisco 94112
18581 McFarland Avenue, Saratoga, California 95070

Publishers and Distributors of Ethnic Studies
Editor: Adam S. Eterovich
Publisher: Robert D. Reed

Library of Congress Card Catalog Number

74-83743

ISBN

0-88247-310-7

TABLE OF CONTENTS

PREFACE

This study arose out of this writer's praticipation in an oral documentation program at the American West Center, University of Utah in 1972 and 1973. In the course of the program it became apparent that a large body of historical material was being uncovered which had not been treated previously. The purpose of this work is to present a portion of that data in a systematic fashion, to analyze it, and to make the existence of the source materials known to other scholars.

The core of this study lies in a collection of taped interviews conducted by this writer with South Slavs living in Utah. These interviews provide deep insights into this group's existence in Utah, especially between 1890 and 1940. In addition, the interviews led to the discovery of hundreds of documents which had a direct effect upon the immigration period. An effort was made to preserve these written records of the group and as a result the bulk of these materials are now available to other scholars in the newly created 'South Slav Archive' of the Western Americana Division of the Marriott Library on the campus of the University of Utah.

The tape collection consists of thirty individual interviews. They vary in length from forty-five minutes to two hours or more, but the average is approximately sixty minutes. Twenty of the people interviewed were immigrants who were born in the old country. Their ages ranged from seventy to eighty-four years. Ten interviews were conducted with offspring of these immigrants. Their ages fell between forty-eight and sixty-six years. Twelve of the informants were Serbs, nine were Slovenes, and nine were Croats. It was the original intention to have included all ethnic groups known as 'South Slavs' in this study. However, no presence on the part of the Bulgars or Macedonians could be detected. As a result the term 'South Slav' as used in this study refers only to Serbs, Croats and Slovenes.

The taped interviews are not intended to serve as a bssis for the statistical quantification of historical conclusions reached in this study. The sampling is much too small to be employed in this manner. Because of the high costs in time and money which oral methods generate, this writer decided to attempt to capture the history of these groups as they viewed it on the tapes. The process of selection was made jointly by this writer and a great many individuals in each community who attempted to refer this writer to people whom they felt would contribute the most to a reconstruction of their past.

Every historical study is the culmination of some sort of joint or cooperative effort, but this study involved almost an entire community as well as academicians. All of the South Slavs who were contacted were delighted at the prospect of the writing of their story of immigration. The degree of community support for the project and community involvement in the project was high. Whatever success this study enjoys is a direct result of the aspirations and efforts of these people. Any shortcomings or deficiencies rest entirely with this writer, who more than anything else, has enjoyed working with and for this marvelous group of people.

Mr. Floyd A. O'Neil, Assistant Director of the American West Center, first introduced me to the possibilities and techniques of oral history. I wish to thank him for being my mentor and friend. Also I wish to thank him for his constructive criticisms and his Gaelic humor, which eased tensions on many a trying day. I would also like to thank Dr. S. Lyman Tyler, the Director of the American West Center, for his willingness to share his wisdom with me as chairman of my supervisory committee. The other members of my committee, Dr. Roger V. Paxton and Dr. Philip C. Sturges, also deserve thanks for their guidance and suggestions. I would also like to express gratitude to Dr. Everett L. Cooley, Curator of the Western Americana, Marriott Library, for his generous support and suggestions.

I would like to extend a note of thanks to the entire South Slav community in Utah and to several individuals in particular. Mr. Mike Dragos and his wife, Millie, the kum and kuma for all South Slavs in Utah, generously extended their support of this project throughout the South Slav community and opened many doors. Mr. John Dunoskovich, Mr. Matt Star, Mr. and Mrs. Joe Chesnik, and Milka Smilanich also deserve special attention.

A special note of appreciation is due to Mrs. Helen Z. Papanikolas, an excellent historian and wonderful person, who took precious time from her own work and assisted me in my own efforts. Her invaluable assistance and support were instrumental in the development of this work.

Finally, I wish to thank Mr. John D. Sylvester for the gracious application of his recognized editorial talents to this work.

LIST OF ILLUSTRATIONS.

xii

CHAPTER I

BACKGROUND TO SOUTH SLAV IMMIGRATION: THE MORMON EXPERIENCE

Immigration has been one of the most continuous themes in the history of Utah. The Mormons saw immigration of the foreign elements of their religion, the Church of Jesus Christ of Latter-day Saints (L.D.S.), especially those from northern Europe, to Utah as the solution to their manpower needs in Zion, which was their name for Utah. As a consequence, they actively promoted such movement for almost forty years. In the same period, opponents of Mormonism looked to immigration to provide the disparate multitudes who would come to Utah and dismantle the monlithic Mormon social and economic structures.

By the end of the nineteenth century proponents of immigration had forsaken their purely religious and social arguments. Instead they argued that Utah needed more labor to man the territory's grow-ing number of manufacturing, smelting, and mining activities. While the reasons behind the advocacy of immigration shifted, the immigra-tion people from other states and from foreign countries to Utah was a matter of importance for certain social and economic groups in the territory. For awhile, immigration, especially of the Mormon variety, became a national issue. Opponents of polygamy (which was then advocated by the Church leadership) identified this marital practice with the American policy of unrestricted entry of foreign peoples.

Opposition to polygamy and Mormonism was deeply intertwined with rising opposition to the entry of all aliens.

Because of this interlocking of issues, the stand of the L.D.S. Church against the demands of the Federal government for social conformity took on a deeper significance in the American social and cultural evolutionary process. The Federal government, in effect, was, in its attacks on Mormondom, repudiating the 'melting pot' notion of American society. It was admitting the inability and the disinclination of the nation's leaders to tolerate pronounced diversity among the groups which occupied the Great American hinterland. The future image of America which it held did not include the sight of many diverse groups retaining their native tongues and social customs, no matter how well integrated they became in the American economic system. While the people of northern Europe and of the British Isles were considered to be tolerable elements in the vision of the future, this was not necessarily the belief on the part of American leaders that they were related culturally or racially, although these ideas were often emphasized. The northern European was tolerated because experience had shown that he blended more rapidly with the 'natives' than did the Slav, the Greek, or the Russian Jew.

The developers of such social theories resided primarily in America's universities, although many others were located throughout the top levels of American industry, finance, and government. One of the most prominent of the academicians was William Z. Ripley, an economist, who expounded the view which was probably most widespread among these people at this time. In a speech to a

British audience in 1908 Ripley said:

> Wherever the Anglo-Saxon has fared forth into
> new lands, his supremacy in his chosen field,
> whatever that may be, has been manfully up-
> held . . . . You (the British) have your
> "white man's burden" to bear in India; we have
> ours to bear with the American negro and the
> Filipino. But an even greater responsibility
> with us and with our Canadian fellow-citizens
> is that of the "Anglo-Saxon's burden"--to so
> nourish, uplift, and inspire all these immi-
> grant peoples of Europe that in due course
> of time, even if the physical stock be inun-
> dated by the engulfing flood, the torch of
> Anglo-Saxon civilization and ideals, borne
> by our fathers from England to America, shall
> yet burn as bright and as clear in the New
> World, as your fires have continued to illum-
> inate the old.[1]

Ripley stated that the cultures and societies of the immigrant

could and should be smashed by the already existing 'native' in-

stitutions, as had been demonstrated in the case of the Mormons, some

twenty years prior to his speech. He also stated that the cultural

inferiority of the immigrants was based upon their non-white racial

origins, an idea which exerted strong appeal in American society

which was directed at all peoples outside of Britain and northern

Europe. These two ideas, as verbalized by Ripley, interacted with

the peculiar Mormon experience and helped shape Mormon attitudes

toward the South Slav immigrants, and other groups, who began enter-

ing Utah after 1890.

The development of the L.D.S. Church's attitudes toward immi-

gration was intertwined with the development of the church's general

structure. The early church leaders constantly attempted to expand

3

their appeal and to increase the church membership and in 1837 they sent their first missionary group consisting of Heber C. Kimball and six others to England to "open the doors of salvation to that country."[2] This and subsequent missionary efforts in the British Isles led to the development that the majority of the L.D.S. Church membership in the 1840 resided in England.

Because the social and economic programs of the Church were community oriented and because the church's prophet, Joseph Smith, and other leaders desired that the Mormons control exclusively the territory upon which they settled permanently, the church leadership decided early to bring the overseas faithful to the area of permanent settlement.[3] When the church body settled at Nauvoo, Illinois in 1839, the leaders decided that a gathering process would be added to the missionary program and in the next seven years thirty-two groups of Mormon converts from England totalling more than 5,000 people were transported to Nauvoo.[4] Unfortunately, tensions were rising among the neighbors of the Mormons in Illinois and violence resulted which led to the murders of Joseph Smith and his brother Hyrum in Carthage in June 1844.[5] It was from this turbulent period that the practice of polygamy among select members of the church was sanctioned and this revelation contributed to the heightening of violence which occurred that year.

The death of the Prophet led to the installment of Brigham Young as his successor and Young led the bulk of the church westward. Before leaving Nauvoo, however, the church body created a mechanism, in the form of the Temple Covenant of Nauvoo, which would allow the bulk of the group to travel together to the West. This covenant established the concept of the more economically fortunate among the group to assist in the paying of costs of transporting the less fortunate members of the group. The covenant emphasized the element of sacrifice and the resulting spiritual regeneration of the group. Also the implementation of the covenant and the organization of people and materials for the westward migration provided the experience in planning and administration that was to revolutionize the future movement of church converts from over-seas.

While the Great Migration to Utah in 1847 provided the neces-sary experience, it also provided the stimulus and the need for a great influx of people into the unpopulated area to which the Mormons were going. By 1850, three years after their first entry into the Great Salt Lake Valley, the Mormons numbered about 60,000 total, with 11,380 in Utah, close to 35,000 in Britain, and with the balance living in the United States, mostly in Iowa.[7] Because of this demographical fact and because a great need existed for more colonists in the Great Basin, Brigham Young sent out the following call to the English faithful:

> To all Saints in England, Scotland, Ireland,
> Wales, and adjacent islands and countries, we
> say emigrate to this vicinity, looking to,
> and following the counsel of the Presidency
> at Liverpool . . . come immediately . . .
> bringing with you all kinds of choice seeds
> . . . and also the best stock of beast, bird
> and fowl of every kind; also the best tools
> of every description, and machinery . . . or

models or descriptions of the same by which
they can construct them.[8]

Because the Saints in England proved to be generally incapable of
transporting themselves to Utah as a result of their financial
limitations the Saints in Utah, under President Young, established
in 1850 the Perpetual Emigrating Fund to provide the capital for
these generally destitute people.[9]   The Fund was to function as
a circular credit device by which all Saints would contribute
what they could to assist in the gathering and then those assisted
would pay back the amount of their assistance into the fund again
so that more people could be helped to immigrate.

The process of selection overseas was very rigid.   Initial
instructions were sent from Salt Lake City to the church officials
in England:

> We do not wish to confine the benefit of our
> emigration to the Saints, but are willing to
> grant all industrious, honest, and well-
> disposed persons who may apply to us, the
> same information and assistance as emigrants
> to the western states, there being abundant
> room for more than a hundred million inhabi-
> tants.[10]

In practice, however, because of the limited church resources, the
money of the church and other assistance was reserved for the Saints.
Being a Saint, however, did not insure automatic removal to Zion
(Utah), and strict measures were implemented to attempt to screen
out the opportunistic, the cynical, and the undeserving.   Between
1850 and 1854, 15,197 Saints were excommunicated from the Church

membership in England.[11]

By 1855, Brigham Young had officially hardened the church's stand on immigration:

> . . . in your election of the Saints who shall be aided by the Fund, those who have proven themselves by long continuence in the Church shall be helped first . . . but be wary of assisting any of those who come into the Church now, during troubless times for Britain, whose chief aim and intention may be to get to America.[12]

The times were indeed troubled for Great Britain and the laboring classes were more aware of this than most. The crowded conditions of urban industrial areas in England, plus chronic unemployment and the wretched living conditions, and the political helplessness of the masses led to political upheaval throughout the nineteenth century.[13] The despair of the proletariat in Britain was a constant which heightened the appeal of the materialism of Mormonism.

The Perpetual Emigrating Fund was the only hope of removal for the Saints in England regardless of their motivation for wanting to go to Zion. Although it was under almost constant financial stress, the Fund attempted to accomplish the transportation of the Saints through three mechanisms: the Ten Pound Companies, the Perpetual Emigrating Companies, and the Cash Emigrant Companies. The Perpetual Emigrating Companies were made up of Saints who were destitute. The Ten Pound Companies were made up of immigrants who could contribute part of their costs of passage. The

Cash Emigrant Companies were composed of individuals who were capable of paying for their entire journey. By the end of 1855, 21,911 Saints had been moved to Utah from Europe through the administration of the Fund.[14] While the beneficiaries of the Fund were supposed to repay their debts to the Fund, the economy of Utah proved unable to provide them with the cash medium to do so, so that the Fund did not realize its expected income from this source.[15]

The journey of the Emigrating Fund emigrants was actually a three-part process before the completion of the transcontinental railroad in 1869, after which time it became a two-part process. First was the trip across the Atlantic sailing in ships, and later steamships. Second was the trip from the seaport to the inland terminus of the railroads usually in Iowa and Missouri. Several companies arrived at New Orleans and travelled up the Mississippi River to those areas, but most of the companies landed at points along the eastern seaboard and these travelled by rail to the frontier. The third part of the trip was from the railroad to Utah across the Great Plains and the Rocky Mountains.

The organization of the ships' companies was excellent and earned the admiration of the immigrants and foreign observers alike. The Scandinavian companies were especially anxious to take advantage of the English language training that their escorts provided during the long sea voyage.[16] Upon arrival in America the company would be met by a number of church officials who had arranged for their transportation to the western railheads, where they prepared for the trek across the plains and mountains. Under optimal

8

conditions the immigrants' journey would take nine months.[17]

The Perpetual Emigrating Fund companies experimented with many different types of transportation on the last leg of their journey. Between 1856 and 1860, because of a shortage of P.E.F. monies, 3,008 of the 8,000 total immigrants for the period were required to walk the 1,200 odd miles from the railhead to Salt Lake City, utilizing handcarts and wheelbarrows to carry their possessions.[18] The people who did this were warned in advance that they would have to travel in this manner, but they came anyway. Between 1861 and 1869 the church developed the Church Team Train concept by which men, wagons, and oxen were shuttled between Utah and the railheads in the Midwest for the purpose of carrying the immigrants to Utah and 20,426 European Saints were transported in this period.[19] The completion of the transcontinental railroad in 1869 greatly facilitated the movement of the European Saints and it was used exclusively by the P.E.F. companies until the end of the Fund's operations in 1887.

The statistics of the Perpetual Emigrating Fund Company are incomplete but Larson estimates the total number of immigrants assisted by the Fund as upwards of 85,000 between 1850 and 1887.[20] The impact of this large group of immigrants was always a matter of concern to church leaders who from the beginning sought to ameliorate the possible cultural shocks which could be expected to occur. These efforts were begun by the leaders of the missionary groups and the escorts and leaders of individual companies. They made the immigrants aware of the fact that they were taking part in

9

a vast cooperative effort which included all the faithful in the completion of God's work.

Because of racial theories peculiar to Mormonism, the people of northern Europe held a "preferred place in the enterprise (of gathering) through being identified with the blood of Israel."[21] The missionary process itself was a selective force used to lessen the difficulties and impact of the gathering upon the Utah community. During the long period of travel required to reach Utah the escorts of each company sought to prepare their charges for arrival with continued religious instruction, language training, and practical information concerning what was to be expected in Zion.[22]

Once in Utah the immigrant Saints were usually charged with duties which led to large numbers of them going to outlying areas to establish new settlements or to older settlements which could use more manpower. As a result of this the immigrant Saints were prevented from retaining their old ties and old group customs, which were immediately replaced by the functions and customs of their recently adopted church. This is not to say that their ethnic and national identities were immediately erased, but they ceased to retain the meaning that they once held in their new role as Latter-day Saints. The building of the spiritual kingdom of God in the valleys of the Great Basin became more important.

The church leaders, because of the centrally oriented political, economic, and social structure of the community they had built, were forced to suppress cultural differentiations to avoid disorganization. That such disorganization would have occurred may be a matter of

speculation, but many contemporary social scientists have argued
that such diversity as was present among the Mormon ethnics, if left
unchecked could have produced a measurable amount of disorganization.[23] Because of the great labor required to make most Mormon
settlements even marginally successful, disorganization of any
type at the community or settlement level could not be allowed.
The results would have been catastrophic.

The order and the security of the Mormon settlements in the
Great Basin, however, were also becoming the concern of the Federal
government. After several clashes, one of which led to the occupation of the territory by U. S. troops in 1857, the Federal government began its long battle with Mormon leaders over issues of polygamy and Mormon immigration activities. At first glance it was
difficult to grasp the relationship between the two issues, but a
quote from President Grover Cleveland provided insights into the
logic which was employed to bring these issues together at the very
highest levels of American government:

> Since the people upholding polygamy in our
> territories are reenforced by immigration
> from other lands, I recommend that a law be
> passed to prevent the importation of Mormons
> into the country.[24]

What had happened was that the Mormons had attempted to find supple-
mentary numbers of converts, especially in Europe, in order to provide themselves with the desperately needed manpower required to
grind out an existence in the Great Basin. In this process they em-
broiled themselves in the then rising national debate over immigration in general. They gained a national reputation and an inter-

national reputation which led to a general interest in their social customs, which in turn led to a great uproar over their sanctioning of polygamy. Anti-polygamy laws for the territories were placed upon the federal statute books during the Civil War, but this conflict and the period of reconstruction which followed it delayed the showdown with the Mormons for more than twenty-five years.

The Mormon press reflected the apprehensions of the community as a whole through the Deseret News, which served as a forum for the Mormons, in which national attitudes toward them, polygamy, and their immigration could be analyzed. The Deseret News took three courses in dealing with national agitation and criticism: first, it constantly reiterated the humanity and high moral purpose of their immigration efforts;[25] second, it consistently separated the issue of polygamy from the issue of immigration;[26] and, third, it identified its trying experiences with other persecuted groups from Biblical sources and contemporary groups, especially the Jews in Eastern Europe.[27] While such editorial policies helped strengthen the feelings of the community towards the 'Gentile' menace it did not create an atmosphere in which a meaningful dialogue could have been established even if they or the Federal government had been so inclined. As a result, the situation deteriorated rapidly after the death of Brigham Young in 1877 and resulted, in 1887, in the passage of the Edmunds-Tucker Act.

The Edmunds-Tucker Act was designed to wipe out polygamy in Utah by forcing the church to give in to the national will. If the church refused it would be destroyed. The act provided for the active prosecution of polygamists in Utah and provided stringent penalties for those convicted, including their total restriction from public office, voting and jury duty. The act also directed the U. S. Attorney General to seize certain church property in the basis of the anti-bigamy law of 1862. And, in addition, the act disincorporated the L.D.S. Church and the Perpetual Emigrating Fund Company. One of the oddest clauses of the act was the abolishment of woman suffrage in the territory.[28]

In the period following the passage of this legislation the Mormon Church abandoned its polygamy stand. The change of direction was embodied in a statement by the then president of the church on September 25, 1890.[29] The situation did not return to normal, however, and the Perpetual Emigrating Fund was not reincorporated because the territorial legislature was forbidden by Edmunds-Tucker to incorporate or license "any corporation or association having for its purpose the bringing of persons into Utah for any purpose whatsoever."[30] Because of this law and because of severe financial problems visited upon the church by the enforcement of Edmunds-tucker, the church officially advised foreign Saints, by 1899, that it was no longer advisable for them to gather in Zion whether they could pay their way or not.[31]

It is not entirely coincidence that the anti-polygamy movement reached its peak at the same time that the first immigration control legislation was passed by the U.S. Congress. Many national and regional political leaders saw immigration as the vehicle which was foisting an untold number of ills upon an unsuspecting America, and

13

polygamy was just one of them. There was a rapidly growing suspicion appearing in the decision-making bodies of America that all America's ills were the result of such foreign importations, and that the solutions to such problems lay in cutting off the source.

The labor difficulties of the 1880's and the concomitant influx of a large number of southern and southeastern Europeans were the "proof of the pudding" that these men were concocting. As Higham describes it:

> The sense of danger pressing on reformers,
> business leaders, and organized labor burst
> forth before (the) larger public about 1886
> when an unprecedented eruption of strikes
> and mass boycotts opened an era of massive
> and recurrent discontent. Nativism, as a
> significant force in modern America, dates
> from that labor upheaval.[32]

It seemed that the Mormon question was peripheral to these and other issues except in the area of immigration, where Mormonism, in its isolated Western setting, seemed dependent upon a continuing flow of foreign adherents. This partially explained the great emphasis placed upon the destruction of the Perpetual Emigrating Fund by the drafters of the Edmunds-Tucker legislation.

The first polygamist exclusion law was not passed until 1891, several months after the L.D.S. Church capitulated (to use Leonard J. Arrington's term) to the demands of the Federal government. The Edmunds-Tucker Act of 1887 had dismantled the machinery of cooperative immigration which the church had built for fifty years, but the immigration law of 1891 directly forbade the entrance of any individuals who believed in or practiced polygamy.[33] As far as can be discerned, this provision of this law was the only restriction placed directly upon those potential immigrants from Great Britain and Scandinavia, and this was only applied indirectly to a small portion of those immigrants from this area through their religion.

During the same time a clause was introduced into the oath required of those aliens who did enter the country and were declaring their intent to become American citizens. It went as follows:

> It is my bona fide intention to renounce forever all allegiance and fidelity to any foreign prince, potentate, state, or sovereignty . . . I am not an anarchist; I am not a polygamist nor a believer in the practice of polygamy . . . and it is my intention in good faith to become a citizen of the United States of America.[34]

As a result of the Edmunds-Tucker Act and the passage of laws designed to exclude polygamists, Mormons of all nationalities and backgrounds were made more aware of their religious identity. The church leadership had, however, embarked upon a course designed to get the church into the mainstream of American cultural development and keep it there. The rhetoric of the opposition period disappeared almost over night and the doctrines of the church and the pronouncements of its leaders blended into the growing nativist movement which was taking hold of the rest of the nation.

The Perpetual Emigrating Fund Company and the missionaries of the L.D.S. Church were not the only institutions or individuals who were attempting to persuade Europeans to come to America. There were a great number of privately run companies created between 1860 and 1890 with the sole aim of providing immigrant labor to American labor markets for a profit. One of the foremost of these was the

American Emigrating Company, which was established during the Civil War by such backers as Henry Ward Beecher, Henry Carey, Charles Sumner, and Salmon P. Chase, in order to import labor from northwestern Europe.[35] Many other similar enterprises were initiated during the same period and they made successful businesses in the carriage of immigrants. Eventually such businesses spread their activities over most of Europe, although they experienced varying degrees of success in different areas. Like the Perpetual Emigrating Fund of the Mormons, these other companies attracted the interest of Federal policy-makers who were desirous of curtailing their activities. Many of them vigorously were investigated and sometimes prosecuted by congressional bodies.[36]

Another facet of Utah immigration began in the imagination of the army commander of federal troops stationed in Utah during the Civil War. The officer's name was Patrick Edward Connor and he sought to increase the size of the non-Mormon population in Utah by promoting mining activities and attracting outside labor to prospect and mine them.[37] While Connor was successful in getting several mining operations underway, especially in Bingham Canyon, the resultant influx of people was not sufficient to overwhelm the Mormons as Connor expected. The following table illustrates the population situation in 1890:

L.D.S. In Mountain West, 1890.[38]

State	Religion	
	LDS	Others plus L.D.S.
Arizona	6,500	29,972
Colorado	1,752	86,837
Idaho	14,972	24,136
Nevada	575	5,877
New Mexico	456	105,749
Utah	118,201	128,115
Wyoming	1,336	11,705

It was long hoped by opponents of Mormonism, both within and outside of the territory, that such an influx would materialize in the nineteenth century.

The Mormon experience with the missionary movement and the Perpetual Emigrating Fund had great impact upon Mormonism and its continued development. For one thing it created a great many memorable events which were incorporated into the short but turbulent Mormon past. The handcart episode in the trek across the plains is remarkable in this respect. Combined with the religious aspects of the missionary and immigration work of these people, the whole era retained a great deal of significance for succeeding generations.

While the church hierarchy changed its priorities in the directions it led the Saints, many Mormon attitudes crystallized in the period of intense Federal persecution and persisted through coming generations, especially in rural Mormon communities. Foremost among these attitudes was the greater emphasis placed upon the role of the extended familial ties as a unifying force in the small Mormon community.[39] While such attitudes had always been strong among the Mormons they received a great boost during the persecution when church leaders and urban relatives sought refuge in the midst of families in rural settings.

Another effect of the persecution period was the creation of a paradoxical attitude toward the role of citizenship and its meaning for the Mormon community. On the one hand, the Mormons became staunchly 'American' after the persecution period, but on the other hand they were careful to direct their energies away from anything that would be considered threatening to their community solidarity from within.[40] The result was the development of a Mormon ortho- doxy in relation to American nationalism in which the Mormons came to personify, to themselves at least, the ideals which Ripley verbal- ized in the quote at the beginning of this chapter. In this way the Mormons destroyed their position as outsiders to the American system. They retained enough flexibility in their nationalism, however, to be able to back away from it whenever it went beyond official con- trol and, as a disorganizing influence, began to threaten the founda- tion of the new church policies.

The formation of these community attitudes, especially the atti- tude towards 'Americanism', were to be of extreme significance in the years after 1890. Then the rural Saints of Utah would come into pro- longed contact with exotic types of foreigners who came from regions of which the Mormons had never heard and about which they cared very little, if any. The Mormons, for so long a persecuted sub-group in the American society, had made their peace with their persecutors.

The Mormons had accepted the new nationalist mood which swept across America after 1880. This mood was based upon the two points of Ripley's speech (quoted on p. 2 and 3) that, first, the new foreigners could and should be bent to the will and customs of native Americans, and, second, the cultures and the peoples which were arriving were inferior in every sense of the word, especially racial. These two attitudes held by the dominant Mormon group became the most crucial elements in the interaction of the Mormons with the immigrant groups like the South Slavs in the turbulent decades to come.

Throughout Utah, wherever the South Slavs came into contact with Mormons, hostilities developed between the two groups. It is probable that many of these hostilities arose out of Mormon attitudes toward southern Europeans which had been formed in the earlier period of Mormon history. The Mormons saw thermselves as the vanguard of American nationalism and they felt it to be their duty to 'Americanize' the new elements which entered their areas of dominance.

The preconceived attitudes of the Mormons toward the newcomers became central to the development of relations between them and the South Slavs. The South Slavs came to resent the air of superiority which marked the behavior of their new Mormon neighbors and the South Slavs rejected it and its meaning. The immigrants, however, never comprehended the basis of the antagonisms which were directed at them.

Footnotes

[1] William Z. Ripley, "The European Population of the United States," Huxley Memorial Lecture for 1908, Annual Report of the Board of Regents of the Smithsonian Institution Showing the Operations, Expenditures and Condition of the Institution for the Year Ending June 30, 1909 (Washington, D.C.: Government Printing Office, 1910), p. 606.

[2] Gustive O. Larson, Prelude to the Kingdom (Francestown: Marshall Jones Company, 1947), p. 39.

[3] Alice Felt Tyler, Freedom's Ferment (1944 rpt. New York: Harper and Row, 1962), p. 94-97.

[4] Larson, p. 40-50.

[5] Tyler, p. 106.

[6] Larson, p. 63.

[7] William Mulder, "Image of Zion: Mormonism as an Influence in Scandinavia," Mississippi Valley Historical Review, 43, No. 1 (June 1956), p. 18-38.

[8] Larson, p. 77.

[9] Leonard J. Arrington, Great Basin Kingdom (Lincoln: University of Nebraska Press, 1958), p. 98-99.

[10] Larson, p. 97.

[11] Larson, p. 99.

[12] Larson, p. 100.

[13] Crane Brinton, English Political Thought in the Nineteenth Century (1933 rpt. New York: Harper and Row, 1962), p. 144-145.

[14] Arrington, Great Basin Kingdom, p. 98-99.

[15] Arrington, p. 101.

[16] Arrington, p. 103.

[17] Arrington, p. 104.

18 Gustive O. Larson, <u>Outline History of the Territorial Utah</u> (1958 rpt. Provo: Brigham Young University, 1972), p. 114.

19 Larson, <u>Outline History</u>, p. 114-115.

20 Larson, <u>Outline History</u>, p. 116.

21 Larson, <u>Prelude to the Kingdom</u>, p. 36.

22 Arrington, <u>Great Basin Kingdom</u>, p. 106-108.

23 Maurice R. Stein, <u>The Eclipse of Community: An Interpretation of American Studies</u> (New York: Harper and Row, 1960), p. 19.

24 Arrington, <u>Great Basin Kingdom</u>, p. 381.

25 For examples see <u>Deseret News</u>, 13, No. 300 (November 12, 1880), p. 3, col. 1; <u>Deseret News</u>, 14, No. 4 (November 26, 1880), p. 2, col. 1; <u>Deseret News</u>, 14, No. 138 (May 5, 1881), p. 2, col. 1.

26 <u>Deseret News</u>, 14, No. 133 (April 29, 1881), p. 2, col. 1; <u>Deseret News</u>, 15, No. 97 (March 16, 1882), p. 1, col. 3.

27 <u>Deseret News</u>, 14, No. 30 (December 30, 1880), p. 2, col. 1; <u>Deseret News</u>, 14, No. 36 (January 5, 1881), p. 2, col. 1; <u>Deseret News</u>, 15, No. 130 (April 24, 1882), p. 3, col. 1.

28 Information related to the provisions of the Edmunds-Tucker Act in this entire paragraph is drawn from Larson, <u>Prelude to the Kingdom</u>, p. 276, and Arrington, <u>Great Basin Kingdom</u>, p. 382.

29 Larson, <u>Outline History</u>, p. 280.

30 Arrington, <u>Great Basin Kingdom</u>, p. 382.

31 Arrington, p. 383.

32 John Higham, <u>Stranger in the Land: Patterns of American Nativism 1860-1925</u> (New York: Atheneum, 1968), p. 53.

33 Higham, p. 99.

34 Portion of statement of Declaration of Intention, by an Alien Desirous of Becoming a Citizen of the United States, U.S. Department of Labor, Naturalization Service Form 2203 (1894) to be produced in triplicate.

35 Merle Curti and Kendall Birr, "The Immigrant and the American Image in Europe, 1860-1914," <u>Mississippi Valley Historical Review</u>, 37, No. 2 (September 1950), p. 203-230.

36 <u>Report</u> <u>of</u> <u>the</u> <u>Select</u> <u>Committee</u> <u>of</u> <u>the</u> <u>House</u> <u>of</u> <u>Representatives</u> <u>to</u> <u>Inquire</u> <u>into</u> <u>the</u> <u>Alleged</u> <u>Violation</u> <u>of</u> <u>the</u> <u>Laws</u> <u>Prohibiting</u> <u>the</u> <u>Importation</u> <u>of</u> <u>Contract</u> <u>Laborers</u>, <u>Paupers</u>, <u>Convicts</u>, <u>and</u> <u>Other</u> <u>Classes</u>, <u>Together</u> <u>With</u> <u>the</u> <u>Testimony</u>, <u>Documents</u>, <u>and</u> <u>Consular</u> <u>Reports</u> <u>Submitted</u> <u>to</u> <u>the</u> <u>Committee</u> (Washington, D.C.: Government Printing Office, 1888).

37 Arrington, <u>Great</u> <u>Basin</u> <u>Kingdom</u>, p. 201-202.

38 <u>Eleventh</u> <u>Census</u> <u>of</u> <u>the</u> <u>United</u> <u>States</u> (Washington, D.C.: Government Printing Office, 1890).

39 Munro S. Edmonson, "Kinship Systems," <u>People</u> <u>of</u> <u>Rimrock</u>: <u>A</u> <u>Study</u> <u>of</u> <u>Values</u> <u>in</u> <u>Five</u> <u>Cultures</u>, Evon Z. Vogt and Ethel M. Albert, ed. (Cambridge: Harvard University Press, 1966) p. 144.

40 Guy J. Pauker, "Political Structure," <u>People</u> <u>of</u><u>Rimrock</u>: <u>A</u> <u>Study</u> <u>of</u> <u>Values</u> <u>in</u> <u>Five</u> <u>Cultures</u>, Evon Z. Vogt and Ethel M. Albert, ed. (Cambridge: Harvard University Press, 1966), p. 218.

CHAPTER II

CAUSES AND TECHNIQUES OF SOUTH SLAV IMMIGRATION TO UTAH

To understand the nature of South Slavic immigration to Utah
it was necessary to understand that it was only one manifestation
of South Slav population movement in the late nineteenth and early
twentieth centuries. White Utah, and America generally, provided
a haven for these people, many others were moving to urban areas
near their rural homes, to industrial centers in Germany, and to
new farmlands in Bosnia and Serbia. It was also necessary to
understand that migration had always been a method employed by
the South Slavs to avoid pressures which threatened their cultural
group's existence. While such an observation may apply to humanity
in general, the South Slavs have relied upon this mechanism a
great many times in their recent history.

Slovenes, Croats, and Serbs lived in the Austrian provinces
of Kustenland and Carniola, in the kingdom of Croatia-Slavonia, and
in the Vojvodina.[1] The Serbs who lived in Austrian lands were
people who had fled from Serbia after it was overrun by the Turks
in 1389 after the first battle of Kossovo and who, with their descendants, continued to flee after the Turkish occupation, especially
in the massive migrations in 1690.[2] These Serbs are known as prechani
or 'over the river' Serbs. The river referred to is the Danube. The

rest of the Serbs lived in Turkish regions in Serbia, which after two revolts, achieved autonomy in 1830. They also lived in Montene-gro.[3] A combined group of Serbs and Croats also occupied the Turkish provinces of Bosnia and Herzegovina, where a great number of them had embraced Islam during the centuries of Turkish rule.[4]

The military frontiers were abolished in Croatia in 1881.[5] These frontiers (Militar Grenze in German, Granica in Serbo-croatian) had been established over the centuries to serve as a buffer against the depredations of the Turks. The occupation of Bosnia and Herze-govina in 1878 obviated the need for the military frontiers. The latter were originally established so that entire villages near the Turkish border could be mobilized rapidly against the Turkish in-vaders, but the concept was later modified so that areas in the frontiers could provide troops for duty anywhere the empire needed them.[6]

The end of the military frontiers coincided with the beginning of the end of the zadruga, or the extended family commune, which was the basic social organization of Croatia for both Croats and prechani Serbs. The zadruga was once common to all the South Slav tribes. It had only been completely rejected by the Slovenes, who did so soon after their absorption into the Habsburg empire.[7] In Croatia the zadruga was looked upon by the Austrian authorities as a sound social basis for the military frontiers. It also served as a means to isolate the area from foreign and economic and political currents which might have upset the military and agricultural nature of this region.[8] The zadruga villages maintained surplus rural

24

population which allowed large numbers of men to be taken for military service without working a hardship on those who were left behind to continue working the land. The _zadruga_ was capable of sustaining this because it operated on the basic rule that its male members could never leave permanently for private endeavors. Missing men were thought of as being temporarily absent, and because there was a surplus of men, anyway, the farm work would still be done.[9] Only females could leave the _zadruga_ and then only to marry into another _zadruga_. There was no private property in the _zadruga_ except for clothing and small, personal items. The land, the buildings, the animals, the farm implements, and the cash were held in common by the entire family and were administered by the male adults as a group.[10]

The organization of the military frontiers had been superimposed upon the _zadruga_ villages and it complemented _zadruga_ concepts and tenets of organization. The males maintained and reenforced their position of superiority and dominance over the females and they were constrained from leaving the commune by military laws related to desertion in addition to the traditional _zadruga_ constraints. Cash inflows from military pay served to lessen the pressures arising from communal overpopulation. _Zadruga_ life was almost comfortable for the militarized peasants. By special laws which only applied to the military frontiers, the peasants were able to avoid certain taxes and _corvees_ which were levied upon other peasants outside of the military regions. Few conflicts developed within the _zadruga_ which threatened its existence.[11]

The real threats to the _zadruga_ system came from two developments beyond its control. First, the general economic situation
of the communal areas deteriorated rapidly in the nineteenth century
and, second, the peasants were becoming, at different rates in
different areas, dissatisfied with the slow economic pace of _zadruga_
life. They became imbued with ideas which ran counter to the continued smooth functioning of the communal organization. Often these
two factors worked together in a particular region but in a great
many areas one or the other was sufficient to result in the dissolu-
tion of the _zadruga_. The Austrian empire left the decision to
dissolve the commune to the peasants themselves and there were always
legal provisions on the empire's statute books providing mechanisms
for the orderly division of the _zadruga_.[12] The Austrians were willing
to let the _zadruga_ degenerate as the Turkish threat dissipated in
the course of the nineteenth century and the military frontiers became less important in the maintenance of imperial security.

In the area of economics the communal peasants were caught in
a Malthusian trap of sorts in which population was growing rapidly
and outstripping the production capabilities of the society's marginal
agricultural base. The rate of growth for population reached its
peak between 1881 and 1890 when it soared to 15.5 per cent annually.[14]
Simultaneously the world market for agrarian produce was depressed
and remained depressed until the mid-1890's.[15] As a result, the
surpluses which the _zadruga_ economy did produce brought little income
to the communal peasants. It was then that the first major wave from
the overflowing rural communal population occurred and resulted in

a dramatic increase in the size of the urban-industrial centers of Slovene areas and in Croatia.[16] Simultaneously limited immigration from Croatia moved into farmland available in Bosnia and Herzegovina (occupied by Austria in 1878). Movement flowed also to Serbia but this was mostly the movement of _prechani_ Serbs.[17]

To add to the economic distress of the Austrian South Slav regions, the Hungarian administration of Croatia after 1867 had embarked upon a purposeful campaign to exploit the South Slavs in favor of their own economic interests. An example of the Hungarian policy was their railroad policy. In Croatia the Magyars built the railroads in such a way that for many years the Slav rail net tied only into the Hungarian rail net. The Hungarians thus afforded themselves high rates on South Slav produce attempting to reach the Austrian and German markets putting their own produce in a better competitive position in these areas.[18] A large portion of Croatia was not even serviced by railroads because the Hungarians declined to provide the capital for their construction.

Beginning with the French occupation of Slovenia, Croatia and Dalmatia (which the French called the Illyrian Provinces) between 1809 and 1813,[19] and the first Serbian revolt against the Turks between 1804 and 1813,[20] many South Slavs found themselves in a radically changed political environment which had cultural repercussions. The French occupation greatly accelerated the Slovene linguistic movement (for which a statue of Napoleon I still stands in a square in Ljubljana, the Slovene capital city). The occupation also gave Slovene and Croat intellectuals an opportunity to gain administrative experience as the French freely employed their services.[21] The

Serbian revolt had much more sinister implications for all South

Slavs. It was a peasant rising against a foreign oppressor which

was eventually successful and all the South Slavs were accustomed

to foreign oppressors. The Serbian experience seemed to provide a

model of action for the rest of them.

The creation of Serbia injected a new element into the world

view of the Austrian South Slavs, especially for the prechani Serb

intellectuals who began to dream of unification with the mother

country, and they put their ideas into Austrian South Slav society.

As relations between the Austrian empire and their South Slav sub-

jects continued to deteriorate throughout the nineteenth century,

more and more Slovenes and Croats began to look to Belgrade for

assistance in solving the political, economic and social ills which

beset them.

The autonomous Serbs, as early as 1871, sought to achieve a

military solution to the problem of the South Slavs in the Austrian

empire. In that year Serbian officers organized and led an armed

rebellion among the Croats and prechani Serbs of the Rakovica sector

of the military frontiers.[22] As Rothenberg states:

> Unrealistic in its conception and execution,
> the Rakovica revolt nonetheless was an important
> indication of a new South Slav solidarity, no
> longer confined by Austro-slavist tendencies.
> It revealed the deepseated conflicts between
> South Slav desires and aspirations and the
> dominant nationalities of the Austro-Hungarian
> monarchy. Demonstrating that opposition to
> German and Magyar rule could unite the Croats

28

and Serbs, the Rakovica rising paved the way
for the Yugoslav concepts of Trumbić and
Supilo.[23]

This new period of Serb militancy saw the creation of a multitude of

clandestine organizations among the Austrian South Slavs, many of

which were provided support by the Serb military.

The Serbs organized the Society of St. Sava in 1886 in order to

stimulate nationalism among Serbs in other countries, including

Turkey as well as Austria.[24] The prechani Serbs founded a semi-

secret literary society in Vienna and Novi Sad in 1867 to circulate

nationalist Serb literature and it was called Omladina, or 'Youth.'[25]

The Prosveta, or 'Enlightenment,' was established among the Serbs in

Bosnia and Herzegovina in 1902 to provide a welfare society with

educational goals to counter the policies of the Austro-Hungarian

administration.[26] At the same time a revolutionary group was organ-

ized in Austrian Bosnia called Mlada Bosna or 'Young Bosnia.'[27] And,

finally, in the decade preceding 1914 there was created the Narodna

Odbrana or 'National Defense' in 1908, and the Ujedinjenje ili Smrt,

or 'Union or Death,' in 1911, which became popularly known as the

'Black Hand' and which was responsible for the Sarajevo murders in

June of 1914.[28] While most of these groups attracted many intellectuals,

many peasants, especially young ones like Gavrilo Princip, the Sarajevo

assassin, were drawn to the ideas and programmes of these groups.

The rising political tensions which affected even the most re-

mote peasant villages along with the exploding population, the

marginal nature of the peasants' style of farming, and the growing

intrusion of money economy all were spurred on by German and Magyar policies of exploitation. With the abolishment of the military

frontiers in 1881,[29] these pressures shattered the traditional

social patterns of the South Slavs still using the _zadruga_ in the

Austrian territories. By the time of the Austrian census of 1890,

most of the _zadrugas_ which remained were "actually single families

with fewer than ten members."[30] In effect, the beleaguered Austrian

South Slav peasant had opted for individual farmplots as an immediate

solution to his problems. St. Ehrlich described the process:

> Objective considerations of the advantages and
> the disadvantages of the two systems-individual
> or _zadruga_ farming-do not play an important part
> in the _zadruga's_ breakup . . . . the people do
> not confront two comparable issues, that is to
> say, two realities. They contrast rather a well-
> known reality with their desires, hopes, or de-
> lusions.

The division of the _zadrugas_ and the transfer of the atomic family

to individual farmplots did not solve the peasant's economic problems

in most instances. Because the plots were small, the individual farm

made the peasant more cognizant of the difficulties which faced him.

Sustained immigration among the Austrian South Slavs began in large

proportions at this time.

The peasants who were the first to divide their _zadrugas_ were

also the first to begin leaving their individual farms in order to

gain cash income from industrial employment. They went to the urban-

industrial areas nearest to them and then to the industrial centers

of the German Empire.[32] In all of the documented cases, such migra-

tion was seasonal and in the years between 1890 and 1900, such employment did not provide sufficient income to the peasant who went through the process. Many favorable reports were coming back from America in letters and in the returned presence of a few immigrants who had gone to America before 1890. Many Slovenes, Croats, and prechani Serbs began looking to America as a place to immigrate for extended periods to earn capital which would allow them to maintain their families and farms comfortably upon their return.[33] The men who formed the bulk of this group were, in most instances, the fathers, uncles, or neighbors of the children who made up the great wave of South Slav immigrants from Austro-Hungary between 1900 and 1924. The majority of these men returned eventually to their farms and villages in Slovenia and Croatia.[34]

America exerted a strong appeal to the Austrian South Slav peasants. Their level of political consciousness confined the bulk of them to concepts of race and nationality and terms like 'freedom' and 'inalienable rights' meant nothing to them. In elections for Austrian and Hungarian representative bodies they seem to have voted strictly along lines of nationality and their representatives were exclusively non-peasant members of their nationality from the urban centers around which their villages were clustered.[35] This was the result of their village ethnic uniformity, their low educational levels, and their self-consciousness over the inferior status given to them by the Germans and the Magyars.

The South Slav peasant villages were, with few exceptions, homogenous ethnic units with all the inhabitants being either Slovene, Croat, or prechani Serb.[36] In Croatia this was partially due to the religious frictions between the Roman Catholic Croats and the Serbian Orthodox Serbs. The educational picture among the South Slavs of Croatia, although showing signs of improvement with the passage of time, was still somewhat gloomy as the following table illustrated:

Croatia

Percentage of Literacy and Illiteracy[37]

Those able to read and write
Serbo-croatian, by sex:

	1869	1900
Men	23%	52%
Women	11%	36%

The discrimination against the Austrian South Slavs was particularly severe in the area of education. Any schooling beyond the fifth year was beyond the social and economic stature of the average peasant, if he were a Slovene, Croat or prechani Serb.[38] Without education the peasants were denied the opportunity to break with the agrarian cycle, and they were unable to free their frustrations except in violent activity which was frequently directed at their German and Magyar masters as occurred in Ljubljana (then Laibach) riots in 1908.[39] As a result of these conditions, America continually became more appealing. More and more returning workers told of the ease of finding work which paid wages that appeared to be a fortune to the impoverished and affluent peasant alike. The pattern of peasant thinking developed to the point that they saw

32

the final solution to their social and economic problems in temporary immigration to America. There they could achieve the economic and monetary independence which could not be achieved in their native areas, and, at the same time, they could retain the benefits of remaining in the places of their birth which meant so much to them.

Those among the Austrian South Slavs who were politically aware could be divided into three basic political groups: 1) those who aspired to the attainment of the reestablishment of their own separate state of Croatia (or in the case of the prechani Serbs, a greater Serbia which would encompass these areas); 2) those who were relatively content with remaining in the Austrian empire, provided they could improve their social and economic position vis-a-vis the Germans and Magyars through cooperative efforts embracing the Slovenes, Croats and prechani Serbs; and 3) those who desired the creation of a 'Yugoslav' (jugo means 'south') state with all the South Slavs involved, including the Bulgars and Macedonians, upon an equal footing with each other. These three attitudes have generally remained at the core of all Yugoslav political activity and they were absorbed to varying degrees by the peasants. Even the attitude of staying with the Habsburgs apparently continues to persist among the older generations. This is reflected in the utterances of many old immigrants, and their references to the more secure times of Franz Josef and the pre-World War I era.[40]

As has been mentioned above, the first wave of South Slav immigration which was to affect Utah, occurred between 1890 and 1905. This group was primarily composed of married men with farms

33

who came to America to accumulate capital which would enable them to return home and purchase rural real estate. They differed greatly from the previous two South Slav groups who came primarily from Kustenland and Dalmatia to settle permanently in San Francisco in 1849 and in Louisiana in the 1850's.[41] The new group went into industrial occupations while the previous groups had gone into farming and fishing occupations.[42] This first wave was drawn immediately to the mines and smelters of Pennsylvania, West Virginia, Wisconsin, Illinois, and Minnesota.

As time went on they spread further and further out, in large groups or by twos and threes to most of the major industrial areas of America.[43] The communities that these men established were of the most transitory nature intended only to provide them with the essentials of physical needs and of the needs of companionship in isolation from the mainflow of near or distant American communities which were in proximity to them. In this period the South Slav immigrants were generally segregated from other ethnic groups. It was a national industrial policy of the time to keep workers separated according to race and nationality.[44] The South Slavs liked the system because they "preferred to carry out their own social customs without disturbance."[45]

The first mention of South Slav workers in Utah occurred in the late 1890's, in the coal-producing regions in the south-eastern part of the state.[46] The first South Slav communities probably were located in this area, but they were of a very temporary nature. Very few Slavic women, if any, came with the initial groups of men

34

and one newspaper reported that women were worth seventy-five dollars "a head" among the South Slav miners.[47] Seventy-five dollars, apparently, was the then current price for a through ticket from the old country to Utah which would be necessary to bring a Slavic woman to the camps.

The South Slavs were gradually attracted to other areas of the state at this time including the Ogden area where they could find employment with the railroads. They were also drawn to the mines of Bingham Canyon, Alta, and Park City, as well as to the smelters of the Great Salt Lake Valley.

The communities that were established in Utah in this dispersion process were almost entirely male. The bulk of these men were from other South Slav communities in the Midwest and East. They were drawn out West by the prospects of better working conditions and, more important, higher wages. The territory, and after 1896, the state of Utah, engaged in advertising in eastern metropolitan areas in order to lure immigrant labor to Utah's growing industrial, mining, and smelting centers, but the extent and effect of such activities were difficult to ascertain.[48]

These groups of South Slav workers were very unstable in that the majority of them were ready and willing to get up and go to another mine or smelter at the first hint of better wages or conditions. And of course when they felt that they had accumulated a sufficient 'fortune' they would make their way back to the old country.[49] A steady stream of newcomers, however, maintained the South Slav presence and formed a base upon which future permanent

South Slav settlements could be established.

The second wave of South Slav immigration to come to Utah was part of the general exodus from southern and northeastern Europe to America in the decade prior to World War I. Approximately 30,000 Austrian South Slavs came to America between 1900 and 1903,[50] but more than 500,000 of them came to America in the following ten years.[51] While the first wave had consisted primarily of married peasant landholders, or elder male members of zadrugas the second wave seems to have consisted primarily of sons and daughters of individual peasant farmers. This is generally true as can be determined from available sources in relation to those South Slav immigrants who made their way to Utah.

A smaller percentage of the South Slavs who came to Utah in this period, but a significant number nonetheless, were the offspring of immigrants who were born in the old country but who resided temporarily with their parents in older settlements like Trinidad, Colorado and Chicago, Illinois before striking out on their own.[52] A good indication of the effect that this had upon the number of South Slavs in the Great Salt Lake Valley was seen in the increase of South Slav names listed in Polk's Directory between 1903 and 1914. While only about fifty South Slav names were listed in 1903, by 1911 the number had increased to more than 400.[53] This list included only Salt Lake City, Midvale and Murray. According to places of employment listed in Polk's guide, the smelters of the Midvale-Murray area were the largest employers of South Slavs in the Salt Lake Valley, and among these the American Smelting and Refining

Company was the biggest single employer.

The South Slavs who came to Utah at this time were predominantly from the Austrian territories. I have been unable to find any indication whatsoever that any Serbs from Serbia proper came to Utah. The bulk of the prechani Serbs in Utah came from the county of Lika in Croatia. This area was one of the oldest military frontier areas and it had one of the largest prechani Serb populations in the whole of Croatia. Many Croats also immigrated to Utah from Lika as this was the poorest of all the agricultural areas of Croatia.

The sandy soil and waterless, rugged hills of this region played no favorites when it came to making the growing of crops difficult. The military frontiers had been popular among the Lichans and the conscription which came after they were abolished were tolerated because both Croats and prechani Serbs of Lika were proud of the military services that they and their ancestors had provided to the Habsburg emperors and empresses.[55] This attitude was adapted by them to their role as industrial laborers in that they felt it only right that they should always get the most physically demanding jobs and, as a consequence, the highest wages.[56]

The bulk of the Slovenes who came to Utah in this second wave arrived from the provinces of Kustenland and Carniola and they primarily made their way to the coal camps of Carbon County, Utah, usually after brief stays in the coal mines in Colorado, especially in the Pueblo and Trinidad area.[57] The movement between

the mining camps of Utah, Colorado, Montana, and Nevada was a result
of the seasonal differences in the coal mining industry which saw
a decrease in the demand for the services of coal miners because
of a decrease in the demand for coal in the summer months. As a
result of this fluctuation in coal consumption and production the
South Slavs would leave the coal camps and work in the copper, lead,
silver, and gold mines in Utah, Colorado, Nevada and as far away as
Montana.

In the period prior to World War I, the South Slavs primarily
utilized the ports of Le Havre and Bremen to embark for America.
The travellers would buy through-tickets. These would take them
all the way to their final destination. The tickets would be pur-
chased in Zagreb (or Agram prior to 1918) if they had the cash. The
money was usually sent to the prospective immigrant by a relative in
America or it could have been borrowed from a thrifty parent or
neighbors in the village. Frequently, the the case of younger men
and women immigrants, relatives would buy their tickets in America
and send them to the potential traveller through the mails.

By this time, just before World War I, transatlantic travel
had become relatively routine, although there was still the possi-
bility of tragedy as was shown by the sinking of the _Titantic_ in
1912. According to more than two dozen South Slav immigrants who
made the trip at this time and who eventually came to Utah, the
greatest hazard that they faced was the banana, which very few of
them had ever seen and which very many of them attempted to consume
before they removed the peeling, much to their distress. Unlike

other southeastern European immigrant groups, like the Greeks[58] and the Italians,[59] the South Slavs were not subject to the abuses of labor contracting and the control of labor agents during their immigrating process.

The second wave of South Slav immigration to Utah from overseas ended abruptly with the beginning of World War I. Internal migration, within the United States from one South Slav colony to another, was greatly reduced by the war boom in the American economy which resulted from the European conflict and which made jobs plentiful and brought higher pay.[60] Immigration picked up again from the South Slav lands to Utah after 1920.[61] It differed, however, from the previous two waves in that a great many of the people, especially Slovenes, came from South Slav lands that had been incorporated into Italy.[62] There was continued emigration from the traditional areas, but these numbers were greatly reduced because of the depopulation which had occurred in these places during the war and which had the temporary effect of easing the economic pressures which still menaced the rural South Slav countryside.[63] The immigration quota system which was implemented by the United States in 1924 ended the last major wave of South Slav immigration to the United States.[64]

The numerical results of the South Slav immigration process are extremely difficult, if not impossible, to gauge. The records of the Austrian authorities for departing and returning immigrants are suspect because of the ease with which South Slavs could and did avoid Austrian regulation in peacetime.[65] American immigration records are not helpful because of the confusion and the ignorance

which the statisticians displayed concerning the nature of South
Slav nationalities and their relationship to each other and to their
Austrian citizenship. Croats, Slovenes, and _prechani_ Serbs were
counted at reception stations as Austrians and Hungarians. The
South Slav immigrants considered themselves Austrian citizens of
the Slavic race. In Utah this resulted in their being known to
natives and other immigrant groups as Austrians, because the Slavs
could not or did not bother to explain to others the subtleties
involved.

Statistics of the Thirteenth U.S. Census, taken in 1910, provided the first reflection of South Slav presence in official
records when it listed 275 Serbs and 2,628 Austrians as Utah resi-
dents.[66] The reliability of this figure is somewhat suspect in
light of Slovenian claims backed by lodge record books for the
time, that more than 4,500 Slovenes (not counting Croats or Serbs)
were residing in Utah prior to World War I and that they belonged
to seven separate lodge organizations spread throughout the state.[67]
It should also be mentioned that the Austrian figure for this
census included individuals of German and Italian nationality but
who were also technically Austrian citizens prior to emigration.
The Fourteenth Census was not much of an improvement over the Thirteenth in relation to South Slavs in Utah although it did include a
county-by-county breakdown of 'Yugoslavs' a term which had come into
use after the creation of the Kingdom of Serbs, Croats, and Slovenes
in 1918. The total for Yugoslavs in 1920 was 987,[68] a large and
inexplicable decrease from the Serb-Austrian figures of 1910. The

40

Croatian immigrant scholar, George Prpic, estimated that the number of Croatians in Utah was in the neighborhood of 7,000 in his book, The Croatian Immigrants in America.[69]

No estimate has been made of the number of Serbs who came to Utah but lodge books of Serbian organizations in Bingham Canyon and Midvale indicate the presence of 220 Serb males in these two places alone in 1918, not to mention their wives and children and the other Serb communities scattered throughout the state.[70] All this seems to point to the presence of at least 10,000 South Slavs in Utah around 1924, with the Croats forming the largest block, followed by the Slovenes, and, lastly, the Serbs, with the majority of them attempting to realize their dreams through their labors in the mines and smelters of the state.

Footnotes

[1] Emily Greene Balch, Our Slavic Fellow Citizens (New York: Charities Publications Committee, 1910), p. 173.

[2] L. S. Stavrianos, The Balkans Since 1453 (New York: Holt, Rinehart and Winston, Inc., 1966), p. 98.

[3] Alan Palmer, The Lands Between: A History of East-Central Europe Since the Congress of Vienna (New York: MacMillan Company, 1970) p. 39.

[4] Paul Coles, The Ottoman Impact on Europe (Norwich: Harcourt, Brace, and World, Inc., 1968), p. 60.

[5] R. W. Seton-Watson, The South Slav Question and the Hapsburg Monarchy (1911 rpt. New York: Howard Fertig, 1969), p. 93.

[6] Vera St. Ehrlich, Family in Transition: A Study of 300 Yugoslav Villages (Princeton: Princeton University Press, 1966), p. 14.

[7] Jozo Tomasevich, Peasants, Politics, and Economic Change in Yugoslavia (Stanford: Stanford University Press, 1955), p. 131.

[8] G. A. Rothenberg, "The Croatian Military Border and the Rise of Yugoslav Nationalism," Slavonic and East European Review, 43, No. 100 (December 1964), p. 34-46.

[9] St. Ehrlich, Family in Transition, p. 32.

[10] St. Ehrlich, p. 34.

[11] Human Relations Area Files, Yugoslavia, EF 1, 167, p. 181.

[12] Tomasevich, Peasants, Politics, and Economic Change, p. 80.

[13] Tomasevich, p. 80.

[14] Tomasevich, p. 153; St. Ehrlich, Family in Transition, p. 50.

[15] St. Ehrlich, p. 48.

[16] St. Ehrlich, p. 49.

[17] Seton-Watson, The South Slav Question and the Hapsburg Monarchy, p. 45.

[18] Balch, _Our Slavic Fellow Citizens_, p. 173; Tomasevich, _Peasants, Politics, and Economic Change_, p. 146.

[19] Stavrianos, _Balkans Since 1453_, p. 264.

[20] Palmer, _The Lands Between_, p. 32.

[21] Palmer, p. 30.

[22] Rothenberg, p. 42.

[23] Rothenberg, p. 44.

[24] L. S. Stavrianos, _The Balkans 1815-1914_ (New York: Holt, Rinehart, and Winston, Inc., 1963), p. 100.

[25] Robert Lee Wolff, _The Balkans in our Time_ (New York: W. W. Norton, and Co., Inc., 1967), p. 78.

[26] Stavrianos, _Balkans Since 1453_, p. 464.

[27] Stavrianos, _Balkans Since 1453_, p. 464.

[28] Stavrianos, _Balkans 1815-1914_, p. 119.

[29] Seton-Watson, _The South Slav Question and the Hapsburg Monarchy_ p. 93.

[30] Tomasevich, _Peasants, Politics, and Economic Change_, p. 179

[31] St. Ehrlich, _Family in Transition_, p. 57.

[32] Oral interviews with Mike Dragos, Joseph Church, and Zorka Bogden; also see C. A. Macartney, _The Hapsburg Empire 1790-1918_ (New York: MacMillan Company, 1969), p. 755.

[33] Oral interviews with John Dunoskovich, John Cvar, John Skerl, Martin Kramerich, Mike Dragos, Tonka Bolic, Joe Hinich, Grey Melich, and Joseph Church.

[34] Oral interviews with John Dunoskovich, John Cvar, John Skerl, Martin Kramerich, Mike Dragos, Joe Hinich, Joseph Church, Tonka Bolic, and Tony Klarich; also see Theodore Saloutos, "Exodus U.S.A.," _In the Trek of the Immigrants_, O. Fritiof Ander, ed. (Rock Island: Augustana College Library, 1964), p. 198-199; H. F. Sherwood, "Those Who Go Back," _Harper's Weekly_, 20 July 1912, p. 18.

[35] Fritz Freund, _Das Österreichische Ageordnetenhaus 1907-1913_ (Wien: Wiener Verlag, 1913), p. 230-241.

36 Seton-Watson, The South Slav Question and the Hapsburg Monarchy, p. 43-45; Human Relations Area Files, Yugoslavia, EF 2, 177-178.

37 Balch, Our Slavic Fellow Citizens, p. 167.

38 Oral interviews with John Skerl, Tonka Bolic and Mike Dragos.

39 William Alexander Jenks, Austrian Electoral Reform of 1907 (New York: Columbia University Press, 1950), p. 200.

40 Oral interviews with John Dunoskovich and Martin Kramerich.

41 Reports of the Diplomatic and Consular Officers Concerning Emigration from Europe to the United States (Washington, D.C.: Government Printing Office, 1889), p. 104.

42 George J. Prpic, The Croatian Immigrants in America (New York: Philosophical Library, 1971), p. 73-75.

43 Prpic, p. 341-350.

44 John Higham, Strangers in the Land: Patterns of American Nativism 1860-1925 (New York: Atheneum, 1968), p. 114-115.

45 James B. Allen, The Company Town in the American West (Norman: University of Oklahoma Press, 1966), p. 17.

46 Eastern Utah Advocate, 4, No. 42 (1898), p. 2, col. 2.

47 Eastern Utah Advocate, 8, No. 15 (1902), p. 7, col. 4.

48 Merle Curti and Kendall Birr, "The Immigrant and the American Image in Europe," Mississippi Valley Historical Review, 37, No. 2 (September 1950), p. 203-230.

49 Oral interview with John Dunoskovich.

50 Balch, Our Slavic Fellow Citizens, p. 455.

51 Prpic, Croatian Immigrants in America, p. 95.

52 Oral interviews with George Pezell, Ely Sasich, Walter Bolic, Matt Star, Milka Smilanich, and Peter Klasna; Membership records of Croatian Fraternal Union Lodge of Bingham-Midvale, Utah (1908-1930).

53 Polk's Directory of Salt Lake City (Salt Lake City: Polk, 1903-1914).

54 Prpic, Croatian Immigrants in America, p. 95-98.

[55] Hrvatski vojnički koledar 1908 (Agram: 1908), p. 60-62.

[56] Prpic, Croatian Immigrants in America, p. 144.

[57] Oral interviews with John Skerl, Mrs. Anton Skerl, Marko Yelinich, Joe Chesnik, Tony Klarich, and Mary Zagar Dupin.

[58] Helen Z. Papanikolas, "Toil and Rage in a New Land: The Greek Immigrants in Utah," Utah Historical Quarterly, 38, No. 2 (Spring 1970), p. 110-111.

[59] Report of the Select Committee of the House of Representatives to Inquire into the Alleged Violation of the Laws Prohibiting the Importation of Contract Laborers, Paupers, Convicts, and Other Classes, Together with the Testimony, Documents, and Consular Reports Submitted to the Committee (Washington, D.C.: Government Printing Office, 1888), p. 40-53.

[60] Morton Borden et al., The American Profile (Lexington: D.C. Heath and Company, 1970), p. 225-226.

[61] Higham, Strangers in the Land, p. 267.

[62] Oral interviews with John Skerl, Rasa Pirc, Tony Klarich, Mrs. Anton Skerl, Katie Star, Marko Yelinich, Caroline Tomsic, and Joseph Church.

[63] Tomasevich, Peasants, Politics, and Economic Change, p. 232.

[64] Higham, Strangers in the Land, p. 324.

[65] Adam S. Eterovich, Yugoslav Survey of California, Nevada, Arizona, and the South (San Francisco: R and E Associates, 1971), p. 43.

[66] Thirteenth Census of the United States (Washington, D.C.: Government Printing Office, 1913), Volume I, p. 877.

[67] Joze Zavertnik, ed., Ameriski Slovenci (Chicago: Slovenske Narodne Podporne Jednote, 1925), p. 510.

[68] Fourteenth Census of the United States (Washington, D.C.: Government Printing Office, 1922).

[69] Prpic, Croatian Immigrants in America, p. 392.

[70] Lodge book, Serbian Benevolent Society, Bingham Lodge, 1918.

CHAPTER III

THREE SETTLEMENTS: HIGHLAND BOY, MIDVALE, HELPER

This chapter is devoted to a description of South Slav settlement patterns using three specific communities. These are: Midvale, located in the center of the Salt Lake Valley; Highland Boy, one of several mining communities once located in Bingham Canyon; and Helper, a town located in the midst of some of the major coalfields of Carbon County. These three communities were chosen for closer examination because they were the largest of the South Slav communities in Utah. Collectively they reflect the major activities in which the South Slavs of Utah participated.

In relation to each community three areas will be scrutinized. First, the pattern of settlement will be reconstructed. Second, the development and organization of community institutions peculiar to the South Slavs will be investigated. Third, an attempt will be made to trace the interaction between the South Slavs and other ethnic groups in the areas of settlement.

The pattern of South Slav immigration as a whole has been described in Chapter II and in this chapter the focus will be limited to local developments. The types of institutions created by the South Slavs include those which are social, economic, political, protective, and religious in nature. These will be examined to the extent that surviving records and data allow. The cultural relations between the South Slavs and other groups were quite complex because they dealt with a great variety of ethnic and cultural groups with whom they had not had previous contact.

In effect, this chapter is an attempt to provide some answers to the question of how the South Slavs molded their environment to themselves and they were molded to it. The effects of these simultaneous processes are both the province of social and immigration history. They involve to varying degrees segments of the rest of the community in which the South Slavs had chosen to live.

This process of interaction is difficult to reconstruct. The materials and the sources concerned with the South Slavs which are available differ in extent and emphasis from materials and sources related to other groups at the present time. Group interactions are therefore hard to reassemble with all the viewpoints included, but at least the South Slav viewpoint should become more clear and coherent.

Midvale

Serbs, Croats, and Slovenes were coming to work in the smelters of the Midvale-Murray area as early as 1890 and in fairly sizeable groups. It was not until the first decade of the twentieth century, however, that the South Slavs began staying for extended periods of time and in greater numbers. This was partially because of the worsening agricultural conditions in the old country and unsettled labor conditions in the larger Yugoslav settlements in the eastern United States, the coalfields of Pennsylvania, for example.

The growth of the South Slav settlement in Midvale was also

partially the result of the dramatic increase in the smelting of copper ores which began to be mined by the Utah Copper Company and others in Bingham Canyon. Prior to 1900, copper was known to be present in the canyon but it was ignored because of the higher profits to be had in gold, silver, and lead mining operations. Also, before 1900, there did not exist a suitable smelting process for lowgrade copper ore.[1]

In 1904 the United States Smelting, Refining, and Mining Company had a smelter in Midvale, or Bingham Junction as the place was called then, as did the American Smelting and Refining Company (ASARCO). The Bingham Consolidated Mining and Smelting Company also had a smelter in Midvale. ASARCO also operated a smelter in the Murray area and jointly operated a smelter in Magna with the Utah Copper Company after 1906.[2] South Slavs sought employment in all of these smelting operations, but apparently the bulk of them were employed by ASARCO and that most of them lived in the Midvale area.[3]

After 1903 a growing number of the South Slavs in the Midvale area were young single men who did not own land in the old country. Many of them had uncles or fathers who had previously come to Midvale. Some had been working in smelters in Illinois, Montana, and Colorado and they were attracted to the Salt Lake Valley by reports from fellow immigrants and through advertising developed by the smelting companies and by agencies of the state government.[4] This group of men lived in boardinghouses or with married South Slavic couples.

The boardinghouses were of several different types, but the most common variety in use in Midvale at this time was the type run by a South Slav and his wife. They would provide a place to sleep, laundry service, and meals including a lunch to take to work in return for a monthly fee.[5] The boarders would sometimes give bulk amounts of food to the woman in charge who would use it to develop the cuisine in a potluck fashion. This could cause some problems but was often preferred by the woman who could not speak English and who dreaded the thought of shopping among the English-speaking elements of the surrounding community.

These boardinghouses were usually homes of two or three rooms which had additional sleeping quarters built on and which provided only the minimum amount of space for sleeping and eating. Very often the smelter crews would work, sleep and eat in shifts. The burden of feeding, laundering and cleaning for these men, whose numbers would sometimes be as high as forty, fell upon the shoulders of the woman, who was often burdened in addition with small children. One woman described her experience in the following way:

> It was horrible awful. You know for awhile I had to carry all the water from a long way in . . . and no dry room. Wash and cook on coal stove and eat in two or three shifts. That was hell . . . woman was slave. That was time I went to see movie and I say if I stay and write my story that would be better than any show or story that they have.[6]

The boardinghouse provided a necessary service but it was looked upon by boarders and landlords alike as a temporary device which could provide a place to live for the industrial workers.

The more fortunate South Slavs owned their own small homes and many did not provide for large numbers of boarders. They did receive into their homes relatives or friends from the old country who were working in the Midvale area. This type of arrangement was very different from the boardinghouse in that the personal tie between the boarder and his host was emphasized. The economic element was considered by both parties, but it was not a matter of livelihood for the host and the boarder was more than willing to avoid the boardinghouse situation. Between blood relations, especially fathers and sons and between brothers, the monetary aspect of the relationship was often completely ignored.[7]

Midvale was not completely constructed prior to the arrival of the South Slavs and other immigrant groups. Because of this land and buildings were distributed on a 'first come, first serve' basis resulting in the dispersion of South Slav boardinghouses and private homes throughout the area. Although the distances between various buildings and homes was not overwhelmingly great, considering the modes of transportation available at the time, this dispersion seemed to have had an effect upon the development of facilities which would be used as meeting grounds.

In the creation of intermediary institutions for social interaction the South Slavs drew upon their previous experiences in the old country and in older South Slav settlements in the United States. The first such device they developed was the saloon, based upon an old country model but modified to the realities of the semi-urban

50

industrial environment of Midvale. Almost every South Slav peasant village in Austro-Hungary, especially in the regions of Croatia-Slavonia, had saloons which also served as inns.[8] They were called biltiya in parts of Croatia. The biltiya served as saloon, dance hall, casino, political meetinghouse, dinner club, and information center for the peasants in the surrounding farms.[9] These same services were in demand in the smelter town and individual South Slav entrepreneurs began operating their own saloons.

There were two major changes in the biltiya as it developed in Midvale. First, it readjusted its operation to the demands of its customers who were now industrial workers instead of peasant farmers who worked seasonally. The South Slavs in the old country had lived through the seasons as a measurement of time around which their existence was centered. Their church calendars corresponded to the cycle of agricultural production. They were forced to begin thinking in terms of hours and days when they started working in the factories.[10] As a result, the Midvale biltiya operated from the early morning until late at night which was a great change from the emphasis upon evening service in the old country.

The other major modification in the Midvale biltiya was its new service as a protective device, shielding the immigrants from the unfamiliar world which surrounded them. In the saloon the worker could turn his thoughts to things besides his monotonous and tiring work. Over brandies, wines, and beer in the Midvale saloons the immigrants could find a bit of the old country among people who spoke and acted in ways which were similar to their own.

Major decisions could be made. The immigrants discussed problems
common to many of them and made decisions concerning getting married,
to become an American citizen, to return to the old country, or to
send for a relative. If he could not read or write his native
language or English he could find someone in the saloon who could.
He could get someone to read his mail to him or have a letter written
for him.

In these informal discussions immigrants learned of new employment possibilities elsewhere. There was a constant exodus of
South Slavs from Midvale to nearby mining camps like Bingham, Alta,
and Park City. The immigrant also learned how to avoid difficulties
through the experience of his fellows who were taught lessons through
trial and error. The immigrant could also entertain himself through
storytelling, jokes, and singing. Occasionally prostitutes would
be available but their employment by the South Slavs in Midvale
prior to World War I seems to have been minimal. The extreme shy-
ness and reticence to discuss sexual matters on the part of the
South Slavs seemed to have generated more repression of demands of
the flesh than attempts at gratification.

In this period national South Slavic organizations were being
organized and they drew the South Slavs in Utah into their orbit.[11]
In 1908 a lodge affiliated with the Croatian Fraternal Union was
organized by the Croats in Midvale. An independent organization
called the Serbian Benevolent Society was organized by the Serbs
in the same area.[12] The Serbian society later affiliated with the
Serb National Federation of Pittsburgh but when this occurred remains

52

unknown.

The primary service of these national groups was to provide life insurance to immigrants so that their survivors could bury them and have cash to operate for a little while afterward. At the local level in the individual lodges the societies served as meeting grounds in a way similar to the saloon. Sometimes lodge meetings would be held in the saloon. The difference between the function of the saloon and the lodge meeting lay in the formality and respectability which was attached to the national organizations which stood behind the lodge. In those early days the individuals who took on the responsibility of handling the secretarial chores of the lodges were transformed in de facto leaders of the South Slav community.

The first secretary of the Midvale Croatian Lodge was a Croat immigrant named John Dunoskovich. He was twenty-one years of age when he took on these duties in 1908, but he managed to impress his neighbors with his abilities and he was one of the early spokesmen for the Croats in Midvale.[13] The leadership of the Serbian organization in Midvale was somewhat more collective in nature than the Croat group but George Lemich (or Lemaich) was one of the more prominent figures active in the Serb community.[14] These men coordinated activities among South Slav communities throughout the state and represented the interests of their fellow lodge members in national conventions organized by the national societies.

The Serbian leadership in Midvale between 1908 and 1916 decided that the Serbs in the area could benefit from the presence of a Serbian Orthodox church. The Croats, being Roman Catholics, utilized Catholic churches in the valley especially St. Mary Magdalena Catholic church in Salt Lake City and did not develop any special need for their own exclusive religious edifice at this time.[15] The Serbs took subscriptions from members of the community and finished building their church by the summer of 1918.[16] Some time during this same year a Serbian Orthodox priest arrived in Midvale to minister the religious needs of the Serbian community there.

The priests's name was Ykov J. Odzich. He arrived in Midvale at the age of sixty-two years. I have learned very little concerning his activities before his arrival in Utah except that he was born in Austria-Hungary in 1856. Within a year and a half after his arrival Father Odzich found himself at odds with his congregation over his salary and maintenance. In 1920 Odzich sued the Serbian Benevolent Society for back wages and rent he claimed were owed to him. The suit named the Serbian Benevolent Society and its leading members individually. The list included George Lemaich, Danye Gerbich, Danye Merech, Danye Maranchich, George Bozichkovich, Milan Pritza, Stanko Gerich, and Nikola Mashich.[17] Odzich's suit was defeated initially but he won a favorable judgment in a second effort at litigation.[18]

The priest's victories in the courts were pyrrhic. By the end of the suits the Serbs of Midvale were thoroughly disenchanted with the attitudes and the actions of their cleric from the old country. Within a year they severed relations with the priest, who was forced to become a dependent and resident of the Salt Lake County Infirmary.[19] The Midvale Serbs did not attempt to get a replacement for Odzich, who died in the County Infirmary in 1935. The church building was maintained and its basement was used for continued meetings of the Benevolent Society. In 1938 an improvement tax was levied against the property because it was being held by a non-religious organization. Because of financial difficulties and the general lack of funds due to the effects of the Depression the society was forced to surrender the property to the city of Midvale.[20] The city sold the church building to recover a portion of the tax and the land was incorporated into the city cemetery.

Despite these religious problems the Serbs of Midvale maintained close ties with each other and even with their Croat and Slovene neighbors. The celebration of holidays, especially Easter and Christmas, was anticipated with great excitement by the South Slav community. Easter was the favorite holiday of the South Slavs and a great feast of barbecued lamb was central to its celebration. Through the darkest days of the Depression the Easter lamb was still consumed as was the roasted pig at Christmas. In the driest days of the Prohibition period the red wines and plum brandies, or slivovitsa, still flowed freely.[21]

The South Slavs made the holidays into daylong parties with eating, drinking, singing, and dancing lasting long into the evening. At Christmas, the Croats and Slovenes would celebrate on December 25 and they would invite the Serbs to join them. On January 7 the Serbs would celebrate Orthodox Christmas according to their calendar and invite the Croats and Slovenes to join in their celebrations. This reciprocal activity was a great source of pride to the South Slavs in Midvale. They felt that they were getting the best of two worlds through their dual celebrations.[22]

The South Slav settlement at Midvale was a remarkable one in several ways. First, it was developed in a relatively ordered fashion with much less social dislocation and cultural disorientation than immigrants generally were exposed to in their American settlements. Second, the South Slavs were able to establish organizations which eased their process of transition to American life without any major difficulties with their neighbors. Third, it served as a place of arrival and dispersal for many of the South Slavs who came to northern Utah. This was because it was one of the oldest, largest, and the most centrally located of all the South Slav settlements.

Highland Boy

In 1898 Highland Boy was a small camp nestled at the end of Bingham Canyon. Residences were located around the Highland Boy Gold Mine and housed a population of approximately 150 people.[23] When Utah Copper and other mining companies began mining the copper ores in the canyon in the early 1900's the population of Highland Boy began to grow. By 1902 it jumped to approximately 400 and by 1910 to almost a 1,000 people.[24] More than half of Highland Boy's population in 1908 was comprised of Serbs and Croats.[25]

The South Slavs in Highland Boy came as miners from copper

mines in Montana, from the smelters in Midvale, from settlements in eastern and midwestern cities, and directly from the old country. A slight majority of them were Serbs and from the beginning tensions developed between them and the Croats. At this same time in the South Slav lands in Austria-Hungary, violence erupted in many areas because of Croatian resentment of the preferential treatment given the Serbs by their Hungarian overlords.[26] The ill feeling generated in the old country was carried to some American settlements and Highland Boy was one of them. Serbs and Croats were present there in large numbers, and they were forced to live in proximity to each other without the beneficial effect of large numbers of native Americans or other immigrant groups being present to lessen the frictions.

For several years the Serbs and Croats of Highland Boy waged a guerrilla war of sorts. The fighting often gave birth to blood feuds and there occurred a significant amount of loss of life and property among both groups.[27] The ill will was slow to dissipate and this early period of ethnic violence affected the relations between the Serbs and Croats in Highland Boy until after World War I. Local authorities were unable to comprehend the violence much less control it. The mining companies showed little concern probably because the miners restricted the bulk of their violence to areas outside the mines. Many immigrants who experience this turbulent period generally attributed the beginning of the end of the strife to a fire which was supposed to have levelled the majority of Serbo-croatian dwellings in 1908.[28]

As occurred in Midvale, both Serbs and Croats established lodges which became associated with national mutual insurance organizations. Also the everpresent boardinghouse was established and in 1907 there were four present in Highland Boy proper. There were 63 private dwellings in the camp so that a large number of both Serbs and Croats were spared the boardinghouse experience. To serve their other physical and social needs there were three saloons, three general purpose stores, a Chinese laundry and bathhouse, and a millinery.[29]

One of the stores was the Serb Mercantile Company which was owned and operated by a Serb named Joe Melich. This man became the leading individual in the Serbian community in Highland Boy and became known throughout Bingham Canyon. Melich was born in the area known as Gospic in Croatia. He immigrated at a young age and came to Utah soon after his arrival in America. He was joined by several of his brothers. Born Bogdanovich, Melich changed his name sometime after his arrival in America. He established a store and a saloon in Highland Boy and the two operations became the focal point of the Serb community.[30] Newspapers printed in the cyrillic alphabet and originating in the larger Serbian communities in other parts of America were distributed by Melich in his saloon and store and he was generally thought of as a knowledge-able man concerning politics and business.

Melich appears, in retrospect, to have been extremely literate and outspoken for a South Slav immigrant of the period. When World War I broke out he became an ardent supporter of the idea of the creation of a Greater Serbia which would include the South Slav lands then a part of Austria-Hungary.[31] From its creation in America the South Slav press had championed certain political ideologies related to the realities of the political situation in the old country.[32] The Serbs in Highland Boy merely adopted a policy which was closest to their outlook once the war had begun. The nationalistic impulses of the Serbs in America had received an original boost during the two wars which racked the Balkans in 1912 and 1913. By 1914 communities like the one in Highland Boy were at a fever pitch.[33]

Melich mobilized the pro-Serbian sentiment in Bingham Canyon and when the Serbian government sent out a call for volunteers from Serbian communities in America Bingham responded with very great enthusiasm.[34] Throughout 1917 small groups of Serbs volunteered for service in the Serbian army at Salonika and by early 1918 the number of volunteers from Highland Boy reached the 100 mark.[35] Those immigrants who were not citizens of the United States were required to register with local administrative bodies but they were not required to serve in the U. S. Army. The local conscription authorities sought to detect those South Slavs who did not volunteer or register and attempted to pressure them into such action by staging periodic raids in Bingham Canyon. One such raid in May 1918 resulted in the temporary detention of about 300 men, the majority of whom were South Slavs.[36]

The Serbs in Highland Boy blamed the Croats in the area for the embarrassment both groups were getting. The Croats felt great reluctance to join Allied armies because they had relatives and friends serving in the armies of the Central Powers, especially Austria-Hungary.[37] In 1916 several Croatian national organizations voted in favor of giving money to the Austrian Red Cross to assist that organization's war relief efforts in their homeland.[38] This action was supported by Croatian communities throughout America and their representatives were verbally abused by Serbs and other groups in America who did not appreciate the humanitarian aspect of the gesture.

In Highland Boy, Joe Melich attempted to ease such difficulties but he continued his recruitment activities for the Serbian army. He also kept in touch with the Yugoslav Committees in London and Washington, D.C.. Both of these groups sent representatives to Bingham Canyon to urge both Serbs and Croats to enlist in the Serbian army. By November 1918 when World War I ended the Serbian community under the leadership of Melich sent more than 200 volunteers to the Serbian army and about 15 volunteers to the U. S. Army.[39]

Despite many problems which developed during the war the Serbs and the Croats were able to develop more cordial relations in the period after the war. This was partially because so many young Serbs left Highland Boy. Once the war ended, the government of the Kingdom of Serbs, Croats, and Slovenes offered free homesteads to the overseas volunteers in the Serbian army. Many volunteers including some from Highland Boy took the land and remained in the old country.[40] The economic troubles which plagued the entire nation after World War I also helped end the strife, because the miners were required to turn their attention more and more to the difficult task of making a living. In addition to these considerations, Bingham Canyon was exposed to the ravages of an influenza epidemic in the fall and winter of 1918 and 1919.[41]

Joe Melich emerged from the war period as a figure of prominence among the Serb immigrants in America generally. As a result he was elected president of the Serb National Federation in 1920.[42] His election was remarkable because he was from a small Serb community in the West and because his opponent was the internationally known Serb scientist, Mikhail Pupin. The particulars of this election remained obscure but it brought the Utah settlements of the South Slavs recognition from other South Slav communities throughout the country. Melich received another important position when he was made deputy sheriff for Highland Boy in 1922. His career ended prematurely that same year however when he died, probably because of pneumonia.[43]

By 1929 Highland Boy had grown into a stable community of more than 2,000 people. In the period following the war both Serbs and Croats built their own separate lodge halls, but they were located in proximity to each other. In the same years there appeared four new boardinghouses, ten new lodging houses, three tenement structures, two movie houses, a cobbler's shop, two schools, four new saloons (and in the midst of Prohibition), three barbershops, and six restaurants.[44] Surprisingly there were only two stores (both owned by South Slavs) in Highland Boy in 1929 while there had been three in 1907. Shoppers in Highland Boy were more mobile and they were utilizing stores in other parts of the canyon and in the Salt Lake Valley through a variety of methods, like the delivery truck.[45]

Highland Boy was one of the few places in Utah in which the South Slavs outnumbered other groups. It was also one of the rare places where the strife and turmoil of the old country was transplanted in tact to a place of settlement. Because of these two factors the South Slavs in Highland Boy produced leaders who exerted greater influence than was seen in other places. Social and cultural decisions were more highly centralized in Highland Boy for a long period of time making the development of the group there significantly different from the experience of other groups in other settlements.

Helper

The town of Helper was founded in 1892 as a railroad camp where additional engine power could be provided for trains trying to cross the Soldier Summit divide going west.[46] The discovery of coal in the areas contiguous to Helper soon made the town the center of Utah's most productive coal mining region. The mining of Castle Gate was founded in 1883, Clear Creek in 1898, Hiawatha in the early 1900's, Kenilworth in 1908, Rains in 1916, Standardville in 1913, Spring Canyon in 1912, Sunnyside in 1904, and many others sprang up in the Helper area. All required the services of a large centrally located community.[47] Helper soon became the center of the coal fields, along with Price which lay a few miles to the south and east.

South Slavs went into Carbon County as railroad workers in the

1890's but in the following years a great number of them started
to work in the coal mines. This early period was turbulent. The
Serbs, Croats and Slovenes who came into the area soon gained a
reputation for being hard working but also hot tempered.[48] As
early as 1903 the South Slav miners became associated with rudimen-
tary union movements in the Carbon County mines,[49] and Greeks were
brought into the area and they served as strikebreakers against a
strike that the South Slavs mounted with Italian miners that year.[50]
The demand for labor in the coal mines continued to grow however
and the number of South Slavs around Helper increased as time went
on.

By 1914 more than 500 Slav miners lived in the coal camps of
Clear Creek, Winter Quarters, Sunnyside and Castle Gate alone.[51]
There were also many of them in different camps and a large number
of them were engaged in businesses of different types throughout
the country. While most of the South Slavs in the county were
either miners or entrepreneurs, a small group came to the coal
fields as gamblers and purveyors of other vices. One of the most
infamous of these individuals was a man named or known only as "Claw,"
because only his thumb and index finger were present on his right
hand.[52] The South Slavs generally did not appreciate the presence
of such renegades in their saloons but they were tolerated.

The activities of the South Slavs around Helper were very much
intertwined with the coal mining industry. The South Slavs became
very sympathetic to the concept of unionization as a legitimate
remedy for their problems associated with working in the mines.

Three major strikes, in 1903, in 1922, and in 1933, were strongly

supported by South Slav miners who became more and more sensitive

to the treatment they were accorded by the mine owners and managers.

The willingness of the South Slavs, and later also the Greeks

and Italians, to join unions and go on strike was looked upon as

un-American activity by the large Mormon community in Carbon

County.[53] From the beginning the Slavs found their Mormon neighbors

hostile and antipathetic. The South Slavs had great difficulty

especially understanding the Mormon racial attitudes. The Croat

and Slovene miners could not grasp the basis of the low esteem

placed upon them on the part of the Mormons for their tendency to

swarthiness.

The Slavs generally had difficulty explaining their ethnic back-

ground to their Mormon neighbors and they came to be recognized as

'Austrians' or 'Bohunks' to the rest of the community instead of

Serbs, Croats, or Slovenes. The Slavs had little choice but to en-

dure such epithets and they came to prefer them to 'darkie', which

was occasionally used. One Serb miner recollected his experiences

recently and explained how he finally left the county after the

bitter strike of 1933:

> They call me everything but white man . . .
> Yeah, sure I leave Carbon County. You could
> die down there and nobody care.[54]

The tense relations between the immigrants and the Mormons was

one reason that Helper became one of the few towns in Utah of any

size which was predominantly non-Mormon. As a result, business

opportunities were greater for Slavs, Greeks, Italians and other immigrants than anywhere else in the state. More immigrants entered

business in Helper and experienced success than anywhere else. The

Italians, Slovenes and Croats often entered into joint business

ventures. These efforts led to the creation of the Mutual Mercan-

tile Company. This venture was started by J. P. Rolando, an Italian,

John Skerl, a Slovene, and A. Dolinsky, nationality undetermined,

in 1924 and it was very successful.[55]

The South Slavs in Helper were exposed to some difficult ex-

periences. The majority of them clung tenaciously to their way of

life, which many felt was threatened, and were determined to continue

to live in the area. The Croats and the Slovenes founded their local

lodges, the Croats creating two and the Slovenians creating three

in the area.[56] They also established their saloons and maintained

them even through Prohibition. Because the majority of the Slovenes

and the Croats were Roman Catholics they had the services of their

religion relatively close at hand. A priest from Price would travel

periodically to Helper to say Mass and minister the other sacraments

to the immigrants.

A large number of the South Slavs, especially Slovenes, came

to Carbon County after World War I. Carbon County was the only

South Slav area of settlement which experienced a large influx of

immigrants in the post-World War I period. A large number of these

immigrants came to join relatives already in Utah because their

native villages were incorporated into Italy after the war.[57] A

large number of Croats and Slovenes immigrated to Helper from the

coal mines of southeastern Colorado in search of better conditions than could be found in that area.

The South Slav settlements in Helper and the surrounding regions were exposed to more stress from outside influences especially strong Mormon hostility than other South Slav communities in Utah. They relied, as a direct result, more upon organizations like unions, joint business ventures, and political organizations to maintain and improve their existence. Their traditional institutions like the insurance lodges and more informal groups like their church congregations proved unequal to the task of preservation in the face of the social and economic pressures which were unique to the Carbon County area. This institutional diversity made the development of the South Slav community in Helper significantly different than elsewhere in the state.

Footnotes

[1] Leonard J. Arrington and Gary B. Hansen, <u>The</u> <u>Richest</u> <u>Hole</u> <u>on</u> <u>Earth</u>: <u>A</u> <u>History</u> <u>of</u> <u>the</u> <u>Bingham</u> <u>Copper</u> <u>Mine</u>, Utah State University Monograph Series, 11, No. 1 (Logan: 1963), p. 17-18.

[2] James B. Allen, <u>The</u> <u>Company</u> <u>Town</u> <u>in</u> <u>the</u> <u>American</u> <u>West</u> (Norman: University of Oklahoma Press, 1966), p. 169-172.

[3] <u>Polk's</u> <u>Directory</u> <u>of</u> <u>Salt</u> <u>Lake</u> <u>City</u> (Salt Lake City: Polk, 1904-1912).

[4] Utah, <u>First</u> <u>Report</u> <u>of</u> <u>the</u> <u>State</u> <u>Bureau</u> <u>of</u> <u>Immigration</u>, <u>Labor</u>, <u>and</u> <u>Statistics</u> (Salt Lake City: Arrow Press, 1913), p. 17-18; also see oral interviews with John Dunoskovich, Peter Klasna, and John Cvar.

[5] Interviews with John Dunoskovich, John Cvar, Joseph Mazuran, and Joe Hinich. Advertisements for such establishments are present in <u>Polk's</u> <u>Directory</u> <u>for</u> <u>Salt</u> <u>Lake</u> <u>City</u> during the period 1904-1914.

[6] Interview with Zorka Bogden.

[7] Interview with John Dunoskovich, Joseph Mazuran, George Pezell, Tonka Bolic, and Joseph Church.

[8] W. F. Bailey, "Life in Croatia," <u>Edinburgh</u> <u>Review</u>, 220 (October 1914), p. 362-371.

[9] A. Steiner, "Spirit of the Balkans," <u>Outlook</u>, 102, No. 9 (1912), p. 534-536.

[10] Oral interviews with John Dunoskovich and Mike Dragos.

[11] George J. Prpic, <u>The</u> <u>Croatian</u> <u>Immigrants</u> <u>in</u> <u>America</u> (New York: Philosophical Library, 1971), p. 125 and p. 264.

[12] Oral interviews with John Dunoskovich and Milka Smilanich.

[13] Oral interviews with John Dunoskovich and John Cvar.

[14] Oral interviews with Mike Dragos, Milka Smilanich and Joseph Mazuran.

[15] Oral interviews with John Dunoskovich, Joseph Mazuran and George Pezell.

[16] Oral interviews with Joe Mikich, Mike Dragos, Joe Hinich and Zorka Bogden.

[17] Utah, Third District Court, Salt Lake County, Case No. 28179, 1920.

[18] Utah, Third District Court, Salt Lake County, Case No. 29417, 1920.

[19] Polk's Directory of Salt Lake City (Salt Lake City: Polk, 1921); in this edition and subsequent editions until his death in 1935, Odzich is listed as an inmate of the Salt Lake County Infirmary. Also see interviews with Mike Dragos, Joe Mikich, Joe Hinich, and John Dunoskovich.

[20] Conversation with G. Bagley, December 5, 1972, and interview with Joseph Mazuran; both city officials in Midvale city at the time of this writing.

[21] Interviews with Mike Dragos, Joseph Mazuran, Joe Hinich, Peter Klasna, Joe Mikich, and George Pezell.

[22] Interviews with John Dunoskovich, George Pezell, Joseph Mazuran, Mike Dragos, Joe Hinich, and Grey Melich.

[23] Map of Bingham Canyon (New York: Sanborn Map Company, 1898), Plate 5.

[24] Map of Bingham Canyon (New York: Sanborn Map Company, 1902 and 1907), Plate 1-13.

[25] Lodge record books, Croatian lodge in Bingham and Serbian lodge in Bingham.

[26] L. S. Stavrianos, The Balkans Since 1453 (New York: Holt, Rinehart, and Winston, Inc., 1966), p. 462-463.

[27] Interviews with George Pezell, Joe Hinich, Tonka Bolic, John Dunoskovich, John Cvar, Milka Smilanich, Mike Dragos, and Walter Bolic.

[28] Interviews with George Pezell, Tonka Bolic, Mike Dragos, and Joe Mikich.

[29] Map of Bingham Canyon (New York: Sanborn Map Company, 1907), Plate 1-8.

[30] Interviews with Grey Melich and Mike Dragos.

[31] Conversations with John Dunoskovich, Mike Dragos, and Grey Melich.

[32] R. J. Kerner, ed., Yugoslavia (Berkeley: University of California Press, 1949), p. 145.

33 Stephen Bonsal, "The Sons of the Eagle," North American Review, 197, No. 1, p. 124-135; also see B. Austin, "Sidelights of the Balkan Wars," Living Age, 276 (February 1913), p. 259-264.

34 Bogdan Krizman, "Serbian War Mission to the U.S.A.," Jugoslovenski Istorijski Casopis, 1, No. 2 (1968), p. 43-73.

35 Bingham Press Bulletin, 48, No. 3 (March22, 1918), p. 1, col. 1.

36 Bingham Press Bulletin, 48, No. 13 (May 31, 1918), p. 1, col. 1.

37 Interviews with John Dunoskovich, Walter Bolic, Tonka Bolic, Martin Kramerich, and George Pezell.

38 Prpic, Croatian Immigrants in America, p. 241-247.

39 Bingham Press Bulletin, 48, No. 16 (August 30, 1918), p. 1, col. 1.

40 Jozo Tomasevich, Peasants, Politics, and Economic Change in Yugoslavia (Stanford: Stanford University Press, 1955), p. 228-335.

41 Bingham Press Bulletin, issues from October 1918 through January 1919, see front pages.

42 Interviews with Grey Melich and Mike Dragos.

43 Interview with Grey Melich.

44 Map of Bingham Canyon (New York: Sanborn Map Company, 1929), Plate 10-11.

45 Interview with Walter Bolic.

46 Utah, Inventory of the County Archives of Utah, No. 4 Carbon County (Ogden: Utah Historical Records Survey project, 1940), p. 10.

47 Allen, Company Town in the American West, p. 169-175.

48 Eastern Utah Advocate, 8, No. 37 (October 9, 1902), p. 1, col. 3; Eastern Utah Advocate, 6, No. 30 (August 16, 1900), p. 2, col. 3.

49 Utah, Public Documents, 1903-1904, Sec. 11, Coal Inspector's Report, p. 66.

50 Helen Z. Papanikolas, "Toil and Rage in a New Land: the Greek Immigrants in Utah," Utah Historical Quarterly, 38, No. 2 (Spring 1970), p. 109.

51 Utah, Facts and Figures Pertaining to Utah (Second Report of the State Bureau of Immigration, Labor and Statistics (Salt Lake City: Arrow Press, 1915), p. 95.

[52] Interviews with Marko Yelinich, Joe Hinich, and Martin Kramerich.

[53] Interview with Rolla West.

[54] Interview with Mike Dragos.

[55] Interview with John Skerl.

[56] Croatian lodge records and Slovenian lodge charters for the lodges involved.

[57] Interviews with Joe Chesnik, Tony Klarich, Katie Star, Marko Yelinich, Rudy Rebol, Caroline Tomsic, and Caroline Skerl.

CHAPTER IV

THE PROCESS OF ACCOMMODATION

In this chapter three central aspects of the immigrants'
process of adaptation to life in Utah will be examined. First
to be inspected is the family, and how its structure was affected
by the immigration experience of the South Slavs. Second, an
attempt will be made to determine what role religion played in
the immigration process for the South Slavs in Utah. Third, the
American political structure's effects upon the immigrants will
be examined and also the effects the South Slavs had upon the
political processes will be looked at.

The Family

The majority of the South Slavs who immigrated to Utah
settlements like Midvale, Highland Boy, and Helper came as un-
skilled laborers to work in mines, smelters, and railroads. They
usually did not bring their families with them if they were married.
The single men did not give any thought to marriage generally until
they were in Utah for several years. When the immigrants decided
to stay longer many of them sent for their families while others
decided to sever permanently the ties with their wives in the old
country. For the single men who were staying longer, the unavaila-
bility of marriageable women had pronounced effects on the future
course of their lives in Utah.

While adequate statistics were nonexistent, it could be assumed that the lack of women of the same nationality was a major contributory force in the decision of many South Slavs to return to the old country. Most of the 5,000,000 immigrants who left America between 1903 and 1911 were single men or men who had not brought their families with them.[1] The proportion of single men among the South Slav returnees was probably as high as the other nationality groups of the period.

The family structure of the South Slavs in Austria-Hungary changed rapidly in the nineteenth century. The extended family, the zadruga, had been extinguished to a large extent. This had a great effect upon the traditional roles and views of the South Slavs concerning the roles of husband and wife, mother and father, and son and daughter in the new and unfamiliar structure of the nuclear family.

Old patterns of behavior and social attitudes developed over the centuries through the institutional framework of the zadruga collapsed in the face of new realities and had to be modified. While very little documentation has been uncovered in relation to this process of social change in this period a study was made in Yugoslavia in the period between the two World Wars. It attempted to analyze this process of change and discover the variables involved.[2] The same factors, plus a few new ones contributed to the decline of the zadruga in the later period as had contributed to its decline in earlier years. The study made clear that what followed in the wake of the institution differed greatly from one area to another and even differed from village to village.

This great diversity of sociological effects of zadruga break-up makes the process of analyzing the sociological effects of immigration on the immigrant family very difficult. The South Slav family was in a state of flux and change in those areas where large scale immigration to America occurred. The family was thrown into general confusion when it was caught in the added turmoil of the immigration process.

The bonds in the South Slav atomic family between husband and wife tended to be weak, especially if the couple owned a farm capable of supporting a family but not of sufficient size to develop surpluses. It was from situations like this that men would emigrate to America without further thought for the wife and children whom they left behind. Seemingly many thought the farm could be managed as well by the wife without the husband as it could by the two of them. Many such South Slav males would remarry in Utah, but many others would not remarry and would eventually return to the old country. There they might find the wife dead, in a relationship with another male, or less frequently, awaiting his return.[3]

The role of the father suffered a greater loss of prestige and importance than any other family role in the Austro-Hungarian South Slav lands.[4] With the inexorable advance of the money economy the individual sufficiency farmer became economically un-competitive. His inability to provide for his family was con-stantly made apparent to him. A 'war' between the children and the father was usually the result of such a situation in the documented cases that are available. The sons would challenge most aspects of parental authority which were usually centered in the person of the father. The increased literacy of the sons heightened the process of alienation between father and son and one immigrant described the situation which led to his own immigration in the following manner:

> My father can's write. He's dumb. That's the reason I get away from Yugoslavia, from Austro-Hungary . . . I wanted to get some education. Can't go to college over there, father broke, poor. All that I learned, I learned from my own head.[5]

The poverty and the lack of opportunities had been strong enough to disintegrate the zadruga. These same forces were strong enough to split the smaller, more compact nuclear family.

It should be stated that the conflicts being described here were basically of an economic nature although they had far reaching social and cultural repercussions. While dislike and disobedience to the peasant father would often be followed by contempt and physical abuse by the sons this was not apparently the rule. The sons, and the daughters channelled their energies into the immigration process and remained on intimate terms with the other members of the family unit. The emotional content of the peasant family relationships was variable but generally it seems that both fathers and sons were hopeful that the children would be able to escape the grind of the cycle in some way.

The movement of the South Slavs to Utah, at least during the period when the bulk of them decided to settle permanently, was a movement of the young. Of more than twenty immigrants interviewed who settled in Utah, the oldest of them left the country of their birth before their eighteenth birthday. Information for large numbers of other settlers from lodge records and cemetery records substantiates this pattern.

The marked youth of the South Slav settlers caused a variety of new problems to develop in the area of courtship. Attempts at developing permanent relationships between males and females were extremely difficult. Competition among the males for wives from the small number of women present in the camps was very heavy. Such competition was often physical and ferocious. Frequent resorts to violence were made by the males and many murders arose from inflamed passions which had developed.[6]

To ease this desperate situation the South Slavs took advantage of every possible means to bring women to their settlements. Brides were chosen through correspondence which was something novel and even contrary to the customs of the Slovenes, Croats, and prechani Serbs.[7] Eloping became very popular as South Slav parents attempted to screen their daughters' suitors in vain. More than once a father and uncles of an eloping bride armed themselves and tried to catch the couple before the marriage could be performed.[8]

The dependence upon letters between the groom and bride led to some very shaky relationships. Often the bride would encounter a childhood sweetheart in transit or renew old acquaintances and be married leaving the anxiously awaiting groom to continue his vigil. Tragically such encounters would sometimes occur after the marriage had taken place and adulterous situations arose. Adultery was not tolerated very well by South Slav immigrant husbands and wives of the period and redress was usually sought by the offended party if it was discovered.

Frequently a male offender was surrendered to the local civil authorities for treatment. The culprit would often give himself to these authorities in order to avoid the rage of the husband and his brothers or the family of the wife. Such was the fate of one:

> Slav whose religious beliefs did not prevent
> him from taking a good thing when it was of-
> fered and who is locked up on a charge of adul-
> tery, who would not escape (during a mass
> escape from the local jail) and who sat around
> two or three hours waiting for a deputy to
> lock him up again.[9]

It was more than possible that this man's hesitance to escape stemmed in part from fear of the offended family which was still in the vicinity.

While the immigrants experienced such difficulties as these in the creation of their families many South Slavs gave up their efforts to find wives of their own nationality. They turned instead to finding wives among the other immigrant groups and among native American groups. In the early period this was very difficult because of the segregated habits of the various groups and

76

because of the attitudes of the Mormons toward the Slavs. The only known cases of Slavic immigrants taking Mormon wives were always preceded by conversion of the South Slavs to the L.D.S. faith.[10] These occurrences were very rare because the conversion process required great modifications in South Slav behavior and because the language barrier made it difficult to imbue the prospective immigrant convert with Mormon doctrine.

Once the South Slav did marry and start to raise a family new problems had to be overcome. The evils of the saloon, the biltiya, and the coffeehouse had been known in the old country and as has been pointed out the institutions were brought to Utah in modified forms.

> The spreading of the tavern and the coffeehouse
> to the village, there serving the function of
> a social club and political meeting place,
> kept many a peasant from home and also absorbed
> an undue share of his income. Conspicuous
> consumption (became) characteristic even of
> the poorest peasant in practically all the
> South Slav areas.[11]

This continued to be the case to varying degrees among some of the South Slav families in Utah. Many an immigrant worker would drink and gamble away his wages before reaching home. The duration and the prevalence of such behavior seemed to have been both short and rare. When such things did occur they caused tremendous disruption within the family.

In the old country disruptive behavior like this, excessive drinking and gambling, had been moderated somewhat by the collective authority of the elders and of the women of the household.[12]

The single Slavic immigrant wife, however, was almost completely powerless in moderating her husband's behavior unless she was willing to take drastic measures. Many immigrant women were both willing and able of taking such action. These measures could take the form of a sit-down strike on household chores or extended visits to relatives in nearby towns.[13] In the face of such behavior on the part of their wives most South Slav husbands became amenable to compromise.

If the husband and wife could not compromise or settle major issues which divided them they were faced with the alternative of continuing the marriage in an atmosphere of mutual hostility. Divorce was uncommon among the South Slavs and the individual who sought one, whether male or female, was usually ostracized by the rest of the community. Slovenes and Croats, being Roman Catholics, had very strong religious strictures against divorce but if a Croat or Slovene couple did decide to end their marriage it was possible for them not to be totally excluded from the group. The Serbs, however, were much less tolerant regarding divorce and they never accepted such behavior in their community.[14]

The pressures which were being exerted on the South Slav immigrant families were varied, but the economic pressure was the strongest. The immigrant laborer in Utah prized his mobility as his greatest possession because very often his livelihood depended upon his ability to move to where jobs or higher wages were available. The mines, especially those producing coal, often operated on a seasonally adjusted basis forcing the miners on many occasions to seek work elsewhere. As a result, Slav miners and their families would travel to copper mines in Nevada and Montana as the situation demanded. Also they would move to the mines of Alta, Park City, and Bingham Canyon from Carbon County when the need arose.[15] Such movement worked great hardships on the Slav families, especially upon the children.

The occupation of mining in Utah has always been a dangerous one. In the first quarter of the twentieth century it was extremely hazardous and lowpaying. One accident in Castle Gate in the early twenties resulted in the deaths of almost 200 men, many of whom were Slavs.[16] Smaller accidents occurred in almost every mine during the period and many a South Slav family was left without any means of support. In these instances the shortage of women took on a positive aspect for the widow, if she did not decide to return to the old country, had no difficulty in finding a new mate. One woman in Highland Boy had five husbands in this fashion as a result of the many accidents which plagued the miners.[17]

The low wages of the miners and the smelter workers made the South Slav families develop many money saving measures. One response was the production of their own food. Every family engaged in the production of wine, sauerkraut, pork sausage, poultry and sheep. Gardens were planted wherever possible to provide a variety of fresh vegetables and fruits, and the woman enlarged her skills by gaining knowledge of canning and bottling techniques.[18] As a result of these efforts and the ingenuity of the South Slav woman, the immigrant families maintained what appeared to have been adequate and varied diets even in the hardest times of economic dislocation.

To supplement the family's cash income individual families often resorted to taking in boarders. The woman bore this new burden almost alone as she was made responsible for cooking and laundering for as many as six more adults. With coal stoves and without washing machines this meant a tremendous increase in her labors and the Slavic woman was not unhappy when the practice gradually ceased. The crowding effects of taking in boarders often forced the children to sleep in the same room as the parents. This created some new problems which the South Slavs were not equipped to deal with. The close quarters seemed to have created tensions within the immigrant children which contributed greatly to their attempts to leave the home as rapidly as possible. Very little information was available on this problem area but this and other effects of crowding must have had strong impact upon the development of the immigrant family.

The immigrant father, after many years of toil in America, attempted to create a better relationship with his sons and daughters than he had experienced with his own father in the old country. Many individuals experienced remorse over the conditions which had been present when they left their villages and sought to avoid a duplication of such events in their own households. Education was stressed as the key to the future for the children. Immigrant parents, especially the mothers, learned much of their English from their children. One immigrant woman said:

> English I pick it up pretty quick, you know,
> American language, and I could count to hun-

> dred dollars, but little by little I could
> speak it pretty good. It was harder if you
> don't have kids, but if you had kids you
> could pick it up from them, too.[19]

The father and mother attempted to teach their children the
lessons they had learned and they expected their children to
teach them what they were learning in the American schools. The
education was looked upon as functional, however, and the idea of
self-betterment through the broadening of intellectual views did
not seem to have great appeal to the South Slav immigrants.

While ancient customs and traditions played a part in the
formation of this attitude, the very harsh experience of immigration
to America was more crucial. South Slav miners in Utah had limited
conceptions of surplus wealth. The conceptions they did possess
were more in harmony with the old agrarian world than the industrial environment they lived in. The use of money was limited to
the maintenance of the family; it was seen as an end in itself
and not as a medium. Savings and investment were alien ideas.
They were considered by many South Slavs to be the 'gimmicks' of
'city people' and 'businessmen.'[20] Education was generally looked
upon as a way of learning the methods of the Americans so that
these methods could be employed by the South Slavs for their own
economic betterment.

The Great Depression and the severe effects it had upon the
immigrant workers in Utah and industrial labor throughout the
country muted the South Slav attitudes toward education in the
face of the new and bleak economic realities. Advanced education,

81

that is, high school and college, became almost unattainable, as
it was for most Americans of the period. The immediate economic
contribution children could make was more important than events
which might have taken place in the future.

The Depression had the effect of transferring almost intact
the work ethic of the immigrants to the first American-born generation. Understanding the causes of the upheaval they were witnessing
in economics and politics the immigrant children emulated the vir-
tues of hard work and togetherness which their parents displayed
in these trying times. The children became immigrants of a sort
themselves as they attempted to become self-sufficient and independent of their own parents' homes as rapidly as possible.[21]

Religion

The church, whether Roman Catholic, Uniate, or Serbian
Orthodox, dominated the South Slav villages in the old country.
Religious affiliation provided the peasants with their special
sense of community and was intertwined with their concept of nationality. The priest had been the dominant personality because of
his association with the mystical ritual and because he could often
read and write. A great deal of the substance of the peasant's
behavior patterns and outlooks concerning his relationship to the
world in which he lived consisted of various ceremonies and feast-
days.

Among the Serbian and Croatian peasants in Croatia, names
were highly prized objects. Each surname had a patron saint

associated with it and everyone bearing that name would celebrate
the saint's day each year. This celebration was referred to as
the krisnoima among the Serbs. The children were all given
saints' names at their christenings and the saints were usually
national heroes of the Serbian and Croatian past. Male offspring
would celebrate the saint's day from which they received their
first name and again, among the Serbs, this was referred to as
the slava. Only males celebrated their first name saint's days.[22]
The Slovenes differed from the Serbs and Croats in that their
names were more reflections of geographical areas, animals or
inanimate objects rather than of ancestors as was the case among
the Serbs and Croats. In many parts of Slovenia for example
particular farms and ponds possessed the name of an owner who had
long since disappeared from the scene. Subsequent owners would
continue to refer to the place in the previous fashion.[23] This
difference between the Slovenes and the Serbs and Croats, could
stem in part from the religious and ethnic homogeneity of the
Slovene villages. The Serbs and the Croats were often thrown together in the larger villages of Croatia and family names may have
been of greater importance to the maintenance of ethnic identity
in that situation.

Religion sharply differentiated the Croats and the Slovenes
from the Serbs. The orthodoxy of the prechani Serbs helped them
maintain their separate identity through hundreds of years of
living among the Catholic Croats. It also helped the Croats maintain their identity because of the large alien element living in

their midst. In the multi-national settlements of Utah this role of religion lessened. With the exception of Bingham Canyon, the old religious differences were quite secondary.

The Roman Catholic Slovenes and Croats found themselves attending Mass with Italians and being served by Irish and Italian priests. The Catholic churches in Utah, however, did not function as 'melting pots' in any sense of the phrase. Interaction among the groups within the structure of local Catholic churches was limited. Important services like baptisms, weddings and funerals tended to be attended only by members of the nationality to which the primary participants belonged.

Two very important religious roles were successfully transplanted from the home village to Utah by the Serbs and the Croats. These were the roles of 'godfather' and 'godmother', or _kum_ and _kuma_ in Serbo-croatian. The _kum_ and _kuma_ were picked by parents of a child who was to be christened to stand with the infant at its baptism and to promise to protect the child and its welfare like it was their own in the event of the death or incapacitation of the natural parents.[24] The _kum_ and _kuma_ would function in their roles at the wedding of a man, but in a different sense than at baptism.

The 'godfather' concept was widespread in the Catholic countries of southern Europe but its significance was in some ways peculiar to the South Slavs and to Slavs in general. Alliances between Slavic monarchs were often sealed by one tsar or king standing as _kum_ for the heir to another king.[25] Many Balkan

84

scholars maintained that the roles of <u>kum</u> and <u>kuma</u> developed out
of the need for mutual protection and defense among the South
Slav families,[26] and if that was so then the tendency was certainly
reinforced within the context of the immigrant experience in Utah.
The number of instances where the <u>kum</u> <u>and</u> <u>kuma</u> were called upon
to fulfill their function was unknown, but there were instances
documented where they did take over support of the children whose
parents were killed.[27]

Because of the need for possessing reliable calendars for
the practice of their religions, foreign language newspapers for
the Slovenes, Croats and Serbs in Utah included an annual calendar
in the cost of their subscriptions. These calendars, <u>kalendar</u> or
<u>koledar</u> in Serbo-croatian, would include both Catholic and Orthodox
liturgical events according to the calendar which each church used.
These calendars came in the format of a paperback book which included articles on South Slav history, political events in the
old country, and other matters of importance to the South Slav
immigrants. While primarily fulfilling a religious need, the
calendars often became forums which advocated a variety of social
and political causes including Croatian nationalism, international
socialism, and Serbian nationalism.

The <u>prechani</u> Serbs in Utah underwent the greatest changes in
relation to their practice of Serbian Orthodoxy, as opposed to the
practice of Catholicism by the Slovenes and Croats. The Serbs went
without benefit of their religion with the brief exception of the
Midvale community where a Serbian Orthodox church was constructed

and administered by a priest for about three years.

The Serbs in Utah took two positions in the absence of Serbian Orthodoxy. One attitude was stated by a Serbian immigrant woman:

> You don't really need a church. A church
> don't make you or anybody believe in God.
> I don't care what religion it is.[29]

Other Serbs felt that it would be better to attend a Greek Orthodox church than to cease their religious formalism altogether. As a result Serbs attended Greek churches in both Price and Salt Lake City.[30] Such an alternative would have been unthinkable in the old country, but the national aspects of religion did not seem as important in Utah.

It is difficult to ascertain the importance of religion in connection with the South Slav immigrant experience in Utah. The Serb community in Highland Boy seems to have maintained its cohesiveness and collective identity more as a result of their living close together in one area without a church than because of anything else. The attempt to build and maintain a church on the part of the Serbs in Midvale seems to have been more disruptive than unifying. The Slovenes and the Croats practiced their Catholicism but their ethnic and cultural awareness does not appear to have been significantly reduced or increased because of this.

Politics and Political Institutions

The immigrants avoided contact with representatives of authority in federal, state, and local government at every opportunity. From their experiences in the old country they believed that police officials and tax collectors acted against their best interests consistently and were to be avoided. Many immigrants had in fact left their villages in Austria-Hungary because of the ill effects of the activities of these officials.

One immigrant told how a neighbor of his had gone to America in the early 1900's then returned to his village and built for himself and his family a new house on an American model. The major novelty of the building lay in its solid stone-and-mortar construction and the inclusion of a chimney, which was rarely seen in that particular area. When the Hungarian tax collectors made their annual rounds in the following year they charged the man twice as much as any other householder in the village. He immediately levelled the chimney in order to avoid the tax.[31] Such negative activities by government officials over a period of many years built up hostility in the South Slav peasants and they thought governments should be resisted.

In many of the coal and copper mining camps in Utah the South Slavs had little contact with American political institutions and public officials because the camps were the domain of the companies which owned and operated them. The miners were exposed to the possibilities of political activity in these situations however because mining interests often attempted to play one ethnic group against another. This was done to prevent the organization of unions.[32] The South Slav miners in Utah were constantly attempting to work with other ethnic groups to better their economic position and force concessions from their employers. This happened as early as 1903 in the coalfields of Carbon County, in 1912 in Bingham, and again in 1922 and 1933 in Carbon County.

The idea of civil obedience was not well developed in the South Slavs and in the area of economics the Slavs were more than willing to strike for what they considered fair treatment. In Utah companies which employed the South Slavs became indistinguishable in their eyes from the political structure which the immigrants believed existed mainly to support business interests. Police officials supported the companies during strikes and local politicians did the same. The immigrants had little comprehension of activities of the state legislature and national congress and so they were generally removed from involvement in these processes in Utah.[33]

The South Slavs did become familiar with judicial bodies, especially the civil courts which they used frequently to decide issues between individuals and between groups within and without their communities.[34] The courts were generally considered to be fair arbiters of disputes. Suits with native Americans that resulted in adverse judgments, however, often caused the Slavic litigants to blame such decisions upon a prejudiced judge.

The presidency was one American political office which the South Slav immigrants related to. This relationship was possible because they associated the president with a king, like the Emperor Franz Josef of Austro-Hungary. To the South Slavs in Utah the significant fact about American politics was the periodic election of a different person to be president. Decisions emanating from the president could only be good. 'Bad' decisions were the result of 'bad advisers' or malevolent actions on the part of bureaucrats. In such a framework of thought the presidency alone, of all American political institutions, remained unassailable. Because of the role of the national Democratic Party in the legalization of unions, most South Slavs in Utah have preferred Democratic presidents to Republican ones.[35]

Politics was generally secondary in the thoughts of the immigrant workingman in Utah because of his preoccupation with the improvement of his economic status. As a result of his frustration in these efforts, the Slav immigrant began to look upon politics as something inseparable from economics. Sheriffs and mayors, they observed, could sell their services in the same way that the workingman could sell his labor. The iniquities and the inequities of these practices were made painfully aware to them, and many South Slavs became amenable to suggestions of radical solutions to the problem.[36]

Prohibition contributed greatly to the formation of South Slav attitudes toward government in Utah and its effect was primarily negative. There was never any doubt among the South Slav immigrants in their various Utah settlements whether they would continue to make and use alcoholic beverages. There was no struggle with conscience over breaking the law. The law was in many ways beyond their comprehension. Attempts at enforcement were resisted by South Slav communities through subterfuge, bribes and other devices.[37]

Their resistance to the enforcement of the Prohibition law had the effect of drawing the South Slavs into local politics. In their attempts to persuade local officials not to enforce the law, the South Slavs became accustomed to face-to-face political behavior and lobbying and even political compromise. They were preeminently successful in their efforts at thwarting the blanket enforcement of the law and their communities remained 'wet' throughout the Prohibition period.[38] The police authorities dropped in esteem because these officials were equivocal on matters like Prohibition, but extremely legalistic in other areas, like arresting strikers for example.

Other attempts at coercing the South Slavs also met with little success. During World War I Slovenes and Croats avoided service in the American army because they had relatives and friends serving in the Austro-Hungarian forces. The Serbs preferred to volunteer for service in their own national army. Only about twenty to thirty Serbs, Croats, and Slovenes from Utah served in the American army during World War I as far as can be ascertained. The draft and the ill will of the native American community did not move them.

In the aftermath of the war the Utah legislature passed a compulsory Americanization act effective September 1919.

> The new law provided that every alien residing
> in the state (except those physically or men-

tally disqualified), between the ages of
sixteen and forty-five unable to speak, read,
or write English required by 5th grade stan-
dards must attend public evening school
classes under pain of fine.[39]

It has been impossible to find one South Slav immigrant who was
forced to attend school under the provisions of this law. Those
who required language training sought it on their own through
voluntary means if they thought it necessary. Most South Slavs
interviewed for this study could not remember being aware of such
legislation. They did not remember being worried that it might
have affected them. The law remains on the Utah statutes to the
present day.[40]

The emphasis upon the negative on the part of federal and
state lawmakers in their composition of immigrant laws also
stimulated the South Slavs to become involved in local politics.
Paradoxically such legislation also alienated other South Slavs
from the entire political structure. This made it possible for
the adherence of many South Slav immigrants in Utah to organizations which advocated socialism. Socialism was not alien to
South Slav intellectuals and the intellectuals who controlled
the foreign language press of the South Slavs expounded such
ideas in newspapers like Radnička Odbrana (the Workers' Defense)
and Narodnia Glasnik (the Peoples' Gazette).[41] As early as 1912
Radnička Odbrana was printed and distributed in Salt Lake City.[42]
Most papers of this type were printed elsewhere and shipped to
Utah.

The receptivity of the South Slavs to socialist ideas arose partially from their experiences as immigrants and industrial laborers at a unique time in Utah. The native Mormon communities were just beginning to feel the effects of the changes in orientation of the L.D.S. Church leadership which occurred after the turbulent events at the end of the nineteenth century. The curious (to the South Slavs) racial and social ideas of the Mormons, combined with their mystical American nationalism, repelled the Slav immigrants. This contact with the Mormons contributed to the attraction of socialist ideas for the South Slavs.

The attraction of socialist ideas among the South Slavs seemed to have remained at the level of intellectual abstractions. The 1933 Carbon County strike was an exception to this. At that time the South Slav miners joined en masse a socialist union, known as the National Miners' Union.[43]

The degree of intellectual and emotional involvement in socialist organizations on the part of South Slavs in Utah was unknown. The federal government attempted for a long period of time to monitor such activities in Carbon County. Since the creation of Communist Yugoslavia in 1945, many Yugoslav organizations in America have been placed upon the Attorney General's list of subversive organizations.[44] In the post-World War II period many South Slavs in Utah who read publications of these various organizations were subjected to scrutiny by the Federal Bureau of Investigation.[45]

Throughout the twentieth century the South Slavs in Utah have watched political events in their homeland with great interest. Many of them contributed money to various political causes. In World War I, Slovenes, Serbs and Croats in Utah supported their interests in the old country. Nationally, in the United States, the Croats were the most active group vis-a-vis old country politics. The Croats formed several organizations which advocated the creation of a separate Crotia. One of the most important of these was the Croatian Circle which was founded in 192 by a Catholic priest named Ivan Stipanovič and several other Croatians living in the United States.[46]

These organizations received financial support from parts of Croatian communities in Utah.[47] These financial activities ended with the coming of World War II when a Croatian state was established in 1941 by Nazi Germany. It declared war upon the United States in December 1941. Croats living in Utah were repelled by the idea of their homeland being allied with Nazi Germany and Fascist Italy.[48]

After World War II most South Slavs refrained from further involvement in the politics of Yugoslavia. They restricted their activities to contributing to war relief funds and to visiting their families and places of birth in the old country.[49] Visits to the old country after absences of forty and fifty years showed the immigrants how much had changed in their absence and it showed them how much remained the same. It also showed them how much they had changed.

Footnotes

[1] H. F. Sherwood, "Those Who Go Back," _Harper's_ _Weekly_, 54, No. 18 (July 20, 1912), p. 8. Also see Theodore Saloutos, "Exodus U.S.A.," _In_ _the_ _Trek_ _of_ _the_ _Immigrants_, O. Fritiof Ander, ed. (Rock Island: Augustana College Library, 1964), p. 199-210.

[2] This study is Vera St. Ehrlich, _Family_ _in_ _Transition_: _A_ _Study_ _of_ _300_ _Yugoslav_ _Villages_.

[3] Interviews with Mike Dragos, Joseph Church, and John Dunoskovich.

[4] St. Ehrlich, _Family_ _in_ _Transition_, p. 89-92.

[5] Interview with John Dunoskovich.

[6] See _Salt_ _Lake_ _Tribune_, 100, No. 173 (April 4, 1920), p. 24, col. 3; and _Eastern_ _Utah_ _Advocate_, 8, No. 8 (March 13, 1902), p. 7, col. 2.

[7] Interviews with Mike Dragos, Katie Star, Tonka Bolic, and Joe Mikich.

[8] Interviews with Mary Zagar Dupin and Caroline Skerl.

[9] _Eastern_ _Utah_ _Advocate_, 8, No. 16 (May 8, 1902), p. 7, col. 4.

[10] Interviews with Joe Mikich and Mike Dragos.

[11] Jozo Tomasevich, _Peasants_, _Politics_, _and_ _Economic_ _Change_ _in_ _Yugoslavia_ (Stanford: Stanford University Press, 1955), p. 167.

[12] St. Ehrlich, _Family_ _in_ _Transition_, p. 55-56.

[13] Interviews with Millie Dragos, Tonka Bolic, Zorka Bogden, and Caroline Skerl.

[14] Interviews with Mike Dragos, Pete N. Stipanovich, Joe Hinich, and Joe Mikich.

[15] Interviews with Mike Dragos, John Cvar, Joe Hinich, Joe Davich, and Milka Smilanich.

[16] _Historical_ _Records_ _Survey_ _Project_ _No._ _4_, _Carbon_ _County_ (Ogden: Utah Historical Records Survey Project, 1940), p. 8-11.

[17] Interviews with Mike Dragos, George Pezell, and Milka Smilanich.

18 Interviews with Millie Dragos, Milka Smilanich, Mrs. Marko Yelinich, Bessie Hinich, and John Dunoskovich.

19 Interview with Millie Dragos.

20 The idea of alienation from the city on the part of the South Slav peasantry is treated by L. S. Stavrianos, The Balkans 1815-1914, p. 80-90. Also see interview with Joseph Mazuran for a view of the carry-over of this phenomenon to Utah.

21 Interviews with George Pezell, Joseph Mazuran, Pete N. Stipanovich, Matt Star, Caroline Skerl, Rudy Rebol, and Grey Melich.

22 Interviews with Mike Dragos, Joe Hinich, John Dunoskovich, and Bessie Sasich. For an anthropological description of such behavior see Joel M. Halpern's Serbian Village.

23 Interviews with Joe Chesnik, John Skerl and Tony Klarich.

24 Interviews with Mike Dragos, Matt Star, Martin Kramerich, Grey Melich, Joe Hinich, Bessie Hinich, and Millie Dragos.

25 Stavrianos, Balkans 1815-1914, p. 94.

26 Tomasevich, Peasants, Politics, and Economic Change in Yugoslavia, p. 182.

27 Interview with Ely and Bessie Sasich.

28 George J. Prpic, The Croatian Immigrants in America (New York: Philosophical Library, 1971), p. 326.

29 Interview with Millie Dragos.

30 Interviews with Joe Hinich, Joe Davich, Mike Dragos, Joe Mikich, and Bessie Hinich.

31 Interview with Joseph Church.

32 John Higham, Strangers in the Land: Patterns of American Nativism 1860-1925 (New York: Atheneum, 1968), p. 114-115.

33 Interviews with Mike Dragos, Joe Hinich, Marko Yelinich, John Cvar, Joe Mikich, Matt Star, and Joe Chesnik.

34 For examples see the following litigations, all from Third District Court, Salt Lake County, Utah: Serb Mercantile Company vs. Mary Melich, Case No. 35270; Slavonia Grocery vs. Continental Baking, Case No. 44865 (December 1929); George Obradovich vs. Joe Melich, Case No. 16932 (1919).

[35] Interviews with Martin Kramerich, Mike Dragos, John Skerl, Matt Star, Joe Chesnik, Bessie Chesnik, Millie Dragos, John Cvar, Joe Mikich, Joseph Church and John Dunoskovich.

[36] Interviews with Joe Hinich, Bessie Hinich, Millie Dragos, Caroline Tomsic, Matt Star, Joe Chesnik, Martin Kramerich, Tony Klarich, Tonka Bolic, and Marko Yelinich.

[37] Interviews with Katie Star, John Skerl, John Dunoskovich, Caroline Tomsic, Matt Star, Mike Dragos, Millie Dragos, George Pezell, Joseph Mazuran, Joe Chesnik, Marko Yelinich, and Tony Klarich.

[38] Interviews with J. Bracken Lee, Mike Dragos, Marko Yelinich, John Dunoskovich, Joe Hinich, Joe Chesnik, Martin Kramerich, Tony Klarich, Walter Bolic, Milka Smilanich, Joseph Church, Joe Mikich, John Cvar, and Joseph Mazuran.

[39] Edward George Hartmann, The Movement to Americanize the Immigrant (New York: Columbia University Press, 1948), p. 245.

[40] Hartmann, p. 245.

[41] Prpic, Croatian Immigrants in America, p. 307-314.

[42] Polk's Directory for Salt Lake City (Salt Lake City: Polk, 1912) and William Mulder, "Through Immigrant Eyes: Utah History at the Grass Roots," Utah Historical Quarterly, 22, No. 1 (January 1954), p. 46.

[43] See the National Miners' Union Principles of Organization and Programs (Pittsburgh: National Miners' Union, 1933).

[44] See Attorney General's List of Subversive Organizations, 1972.

[45] Interviews with Matt Star, Joe Chesnik, and John Skerl.

[46] Prpic, Croatian Immigrants in America, p. 269.

[47] Interviews with John Dunoskovich, Matt Star, Martin Kramerich, and Tony Klarich.

[48] Interviews with John Dunoskovich, Rasa Pirc, Peter and Ely Klasna, and Katie Star.

[49] Interviews with Mike Dragos, Walter Bolic, Zorka Bogden, George Pezell, Joseph Mazuran, Peter and Ely Klasna, Joe Hinich, and Joe Chesnik.

CHAPTER V

CONCLUSIONS

An attempt has been made in this inquiry to reconstruct the immigration experiences of the South Slavs in Utah between 1890 and 1940. This writer believes that this has been accomplished. It is also this writer's belief that significant data has been presented which relates to other aspects of his torical invest- igation.

From the initiation of this study it was assumed that the peculiar history of the Mormons had a definite effect upon inter- cultural relations between them and the South Slavs. The L.D.S. community in Utah is something unique in American history and it has experienced a somewhat different past than other peoples in other parts of America. The Slovenes, Croats and Serbs came to Utah and faced a whole array of problems which differed signi- ficantly from those they faced in other settlements like the larger urban areas of Cleveland, Chicago and Pittsburgh.

This writer was not aware, however, of the importance of the role which immigration played in the formation of Mormon society in Utah. The methods which the L.D.S. Church leadership used to ameliorate the problems of accommodating large groups of people with diverse cultural backgrounds had a strong influence upon the development of social attitudes and cultural values. While this process was modified because of the difficulties the church encountered with the federal government, it seems to have been of crucial importance in the crystallization of attitudes and behavior among the Mormons which just preceded the arrival of the South Slav immigrants.

The formation of Mormon racial attitudes toward ethnics like the South Slavs seems to have stemmed in part from the missionary and immigration period. The Mormon preference for converts of North European stock was based on religious beliefs. This led to a growth of a sense of personal and community exclusiveness to which other elements of Mormon doctrine, which outlined their special mission in other ways, also contributed.

The racial attitudes which the Mormons expressed in speech and behavior to the South Slavs produced friction. These racial attitudes combined with the Mormon concepts of collective social behavior led to extreme competition between the two groups in those places where both were present in sufficient numbers. The resulting conflicts had an unknown effect upon the Mormons, but the effects upon the South Slavs are recognizable and have been detailed in previous chapters.

It should be remembered that the decision to immigrate from the South Slav lands was preceded by a general collapse of traditionally accepted institutions and forms of behavior. In many ways the immigrants were rejecting their past so that they could improve their economic status. When the South Slavs were faced with the hostility and the solidarity of the Mormons, however, many immigrants appear to have experienced doubts concerning the wisdom of any total rejection of their past which they might have contemplated.

It was partially because of this that the South Slavs in Utah maintained their elaborate kinship systems in the early years and the importance of the _kum_ or godfather role. It was also a result of Mormon attitudes that contempt and hostility were generally felt for the Mormons by the South Slavs. The South Slavs disliked what they believed to be a certain amount of hypocrisy between Mormon belief and Mormon behavior. The South Slavs felt hostility toward the Mormons because of the racial slurs which the Mormons cast upon them and because the Mormon communities often supported economic interests which were diametrically opposed to the economic interests of the South Slav workingmen.

It would be of interest to see if such conflicts were generated between other resident groups and South Slav immigrants in other parts of America. This could assist in the determination of how much of the conflict between Mormons and South Slavs was the result of purely local factors or whether such hostilities could be associated with more general tensions which might be associated with the process of immigration.

The tense relations between the South Slavs and the Mormons should not be overstressed or distorted. While mutual hostilities and mutual contempt were often evidenced it should be borne in mind that those South Slavs studied still preferred to locate in Utah rather than in other industrial areas in the rest of the United States. Analysis of this phenomenon requires some comparative study between the South Slav settlements in Utah and those which were located in other parts of the country. An area which would lend itself to such study is the Trinidad-Pueblo area of southeastern Colorado where significant South Slav populations were present.

It can be seen from the Mormon experience prior to the arrival of the South Slavs that immigration has played a central role in the course of Utah history since the late eighteen forties. It is difficult to comprehend the diversity which immigration brought to Utah society. Naturalization records in Carbon County between 1894 and 1938 listed more than twenty-five ethnic and nationality groups from Europe, the Near and Middle East, the Orient, and Latin America. While such diversity was present it was on a small scale.

Relations between the different South Slav groups and other immigrant groups were generally amiable. These groups did not, however, freely intermingle within any sort of 'melting pot' framework. The retention of the exclusive identity of each group is a remarkable feature of the total immigration picture in Utah. This includes, to a lesser degree, even the ethnic groups which immigrated to Utah under the auspices of the L.D.S. Church.

Amicable relations between the ethnic groups may also have stemmed in part from the presence of a common threat. This common threat was the cohesive Mormon community which tended to deal with non-Mormon communities in similar ways. This development explains in part the relative closeness of prechani Serbs and Greeks on one hand and between the Slovenes and Croats with the Italians on the other hand. It should be remembered that it was only in those areas where Mormons were not present in large numbers that old conflicts broke out between the Serbs and the Croats, as was the South Slav experience in Highland Boy. In Utah it seems that the presence of a dominant group, the Mormons, contributed to a lateral identification among the immigrant groups. This tendency, however, does not appear to have led to an abolition of separate ethnic identities.

The causes of South Slav immigration to America were products of the unique cultural and historical experience of the South Slavs. The decision to immigrate seems to have been a voluntary one. It also appears to have been an individual one. However, the settlement patterns of the South Slavs in Utah reveals that people from the same villages and regions in the old country tended to settle in new places in Utah with people they had known or to whom they were related in the old country.

South Slav immigration to Utah, then, was an individual movement only to the extent that modes of transportation tended to individualize the process. Whereas in the eighteenth and nineteenth centuries the movement of immigrants to America had tended to be a group phenomenon, especially in transit, it was a group phenomenon among the South Slavs except in transit. What literature that has been produced relative to the South Slav immigration has tended to ignore this facet of this group's movement with the result that economic motivation of individual immigrants has been

the primary area of emphasis in the explanation of South Slav
immigrant behavior.

Economic considerations were of course of primary importance
in the immigration process, but at least in Utah kinship ties and
regional identification played a much greater role in the decision
to settle in particular places. While higher wages in Utah
attracted the South Slavs, even more attractive was the prospect
of living and working with the people they had known or were
familiar with in the old country.

Because of a dependency upon kinship ties, ties which had
been rejected as they were embodied in the zadruga, the South Slavs
found themselves reestablishing a modified zadruga in the form of
the boardinghouse. Immigration therefore became the collective
activity among the South Slavs in Utah in a manner similar to
other immigrant groups in other contexts of American history.
This development partially explains why South Slav communities
sprang up in Utah, and why these people collected themselves there
rather than in larger settlements in the eastern United States and
instead of other countries like Brazil, Australia or even Russia.

While immigration was of a collective nature for the South
Slavs who came to Utah, it was not a rigid system. Great individual freedom which resulted from the zadruga break-up was retained. The constraints which held the individual South Slav in
loyalty to other members of the group were not reinforced with
powerful sanctions as had been the case in the extended family.
The constraints among the immigrants were more individualized and

they depended upon the individual's view of his relationship to other members of his ethnic group. This dichotomy between the behavior of the individual and that of the group is the most distinctive facet of South Slav cultural development in Utah.

For the South Slavs who arrived in Utah transportation to America and to Utah followed definite patterns. Throughout the nineteenth century and before the beginning of World War I, the South Slavs primarily utilized the ports of Le Havre and Bremen for embarkation to America. Why these ports were used to such an overwhelming degree is a question which remains unanswered. Following World War I the ports of the Adriatic Sea, especially Trieste, were used predominantly by the South Slav immigrants. This movement in part stems from the new political configurations which came into existence in the postwar political settlements.

Once in America the immigrants primarily depended upon railroads to carry them to their final place of settlement in Utah. Which railroads were used and the cost of this usage remains unknown, but the railroads seem to have played an important part in the bringing of South Slavs to Utah.

The role of national South Slav organizations, like the insurance lodges, remains obscure. This study, because of a lack of access to records of these institutions, has concentrated upon establishing what the attitudes of the local communities were toward the local organizations. Data from oral sources states that such organizations actually financed the transportation of South Slav immigrants to America, but very few South Slav immigrants maintained that they personally benefited from such assistance.

The national organizations of the South Slavs are worthy of investigation. Their records and their publications form an important part of the heritage of the South Slav immigrant movement. The tendency toward mass participation on the part of the South Slavs in Utah in these organizations tends to make a better understanding of them particularly important.

In a similar manner the foreign language publications of the South Slavs and other groups have been neglected. This neglect has led to a general assumption even among immigration historians that the written communication played a small part in the immigration experiences of the southern European immigrants. This writer feels that this attitude does a disservice to attempts at obtaining a greater understanding of the immigrant and his world. Further study of this question is necessary before the degree of importance of the written word in the life of the immigrant can be ascertained.

The adaptation of the South Slavs to their environment in Utah has been and continues to be a dynamic process. There does not appear to be a 'magic' moment which marks the transition of the immigrant into a non-immigrant status. The process of adopting and discarding different forms of behavior and different attitudes among the South Slavs in Utah does not appear to have been an irrevocable process. Just as the South Slavs rejected the zadruga and then recreated a modified form of it in their boardinghouses, so they have done with other values, behavior and institutions in their environment.

The dynamic nature of this activity is illustrated in the activities of the Slovenes and Croats in Helper, Utah since the early 1950's. A sort of 'mini-renaissance' has occurred among the South Slavs of the area. This process has resulted in the South Slav community creating a new institution, the Slovenian National Home, to serve as the social center of both the Slovene and Croat communities in the Helper area.

The use of the national home is nothing new to Slavs in America but it is new to the Helper area. The movement to create this institution is a response on the part of many first and second generation Slovenes and Croats to replace the biltiya and the local lodge with a more useful and responsive community center. Both the biltiya and the local insurance lodge have declined in importance among the local South Slavs and the national home was chosen by them, collectively, as a means of continuing the traditions which both institutions once embodied. The 'home' is actually a private club which functions as a bar, restaurant, meeting hall and dance hall. It was created and has been maintained through personal contributions of money and time on the part of the Slovenes and Croats in the area. This resurgence of social activity on the part of the South Slavs in Helper has led to the town becoming the social center of the South Slavs in parts of Utah, Colorado, New Mexico and even Montana. Celebrations of holidays, like Christmas and Easter, held in the Slovenian National Home, or sponsored by the members in other parts of the area are well attended by South

Slavs from other places throughout the Intermountain area.

This type of activity on the part of the surviving immigrants and their descendants is seen everywhere they continue to live in communities in Utah. While it is not immediately noticeable to the untrained eye, it becomes obvious to the investigator. This continued behavior along ethnic lines shows that the immigrant tradition is still a potent social force. It also facilitates historical investigations like this one.

Face-to-face contacts between this writer and the immigrants who have lived through the process of immigration was made possible through the continued survival of local institutions and channels of communication within the separate immigrant communities. The rapid and systematic collection of oral testimony was also facilitated by the fact that these same local bodies also werve as repositories for much of the written records pertaining to South Slav immigration in Utah which still exists.

What the future holds for the continued existence of the South Slav ethnic communities in Utah is difficult to ascertain, Many factors seem to indicate that eventually these groups will be overwhelmed by the atomizing effects of modern American society and by disruptive tendencies within the groups themselves. Simultaneously, however, these pressures tend to work to restore the need for community identification in the minds of the South Slav ethnics.

The growing awareness of racial and ethnic diversity which has spread across America since the late 1950's has affected the South

Slavs in Utah and throughout the nation. Third generation descendants of the immigrants have taken active interest in the peculiarities of their past to help them understand their own relationships to the world in which they live and this interest has led in turn to attempts on their part to understand the singular activities of their parents and grandparents.

It is paradoxical, but the same forces which seem to be driving individuals away from group affiliations seems at the same time to be driving them together. Ethnic interaction, however, does not simply represent celebrating together. It is related to the process which affects all human beings and that is the process of relating to and coping with the reality that each individual finds himself or herself existing in. The idea of ethnic identity is but one means by which people attempt to accomplish the successful living of their lives in an atmosphere which is comfortable for them.

For the South Slavs in Utah, their dependence upon blood ties and their own peculiar kinship system are their methods of coming to grips with what they see as the impersonal process with which modern America has come to be identified among them. While the future is still unclear, the past is more apparent. The South Slavs have maintained their sense of ethnic exclusiveness in the years that have passed since their arrival in Utah.

This retention of ethnic identity has occurred even though the South Slav settlements in Utah are among the smallest South Slav communities in America. The continued cohesiveness of their communities belies their numerical weakness. Despite the fact that they were generally identified as 'Austrians' and 'Bohunks', the South Slavs maintained their separate ethnic identities and a lot of their cultural heritage. That which they have discarded was discarded in order for them to function effectively in the new economic environment in which they placed themselves.

Economic behavior played a very great role in the past cultural activity of the South Slavs in Utah. Their choice of occupations and the choice of occupations on the part of their children determined to a large extent what aspects of the cultural heritage would be retained. The more time and effort spent in economic pursuits the less time and effort was left over for the preservation of cultural and social institutions and behavioral patterns.

Economic activity among the children of the immigrants was extremely important in the shaping of this pattern of cultural transmission. Generally, it appears that the offspring of the immigrants accepted the cultural legacy of their parents according to the degree that they imitated their parents in terms of occupation and place of residence. If the children remained in the same area and went to work in the same occupations as the parents, the South Slav communities proved more resilient and dynamic. If the children left the area of original settlement, the process of cultural transmission was negatively affected.

The offspring of the immigrants who left the communities which their parents had created became immigrants in a sense similar to their parents. They partially rejected the values and life style of their parents and sought to improve their own economic position in society. The permanence of this rejection is a matter for conjecture, but it forms the basic threat to the continued existence of the South Slav ethnic enclaves in Utah. If the offspring continue to exchange the security and warmth of their ethnic communities for the mobility and competition of the American economic system then the South Slav communities will eventually cease to function.

The story of South Slav immigration to Utah forms an important part of the story of Utah's entry into the twentieth century. Their almost total involvement in the industrialization process in the early years of this century gives them and other immigrant groups who came before and after them an important niche in the history of this turbulent and exciting period. The story of the South Slavs in Utah also forms an important part in the overall story of general immigration to America.

BIBLIOGRAPHY

Books

Allen, James B. The Company Town in the American West. Norman: University of Oklahoma Press, 1966.

Ander, O. Fritiof, Ed. In the Trek of the Immigrants. Rock Island: Augustana College Library, 1964.

Arrington, Leonard J. Great Basin Kingdom. Lincoln: University of Nebraska Press, 1958.

Balch, Emily Greene. Our Slavic Fellow Citizens. New York: Charities Publications, 1910.

Borden, Morton, et al. The American Profile. Lexington: D.C. Heath and Company, 1970.

Brinton, Crane. English Political Thought in the Nineteenth Century. 1933 rpt. New York: Harper and Row, 1962.

Coles, Paul. The Ottoman Impact on Europe. Norwich: Harcourt, and World, Inc., 1968.

Eterovich, Adam S. Yugoslav Survey of California, Nevada, Arizona and the South. San Francisco: R. and E Associates, 1971.

Freund, Fritz. Das österreichische Asgeordnetenhaus 1907-1913. Wien: Wiener Verlag, 1913.

Hartmann, Edward G. The Movement to Americanize the Immigrant. New York: Columbia University Press, 1948.

Higham, John. Stranger in the Land: Patterns of American Nativism 1860-1925. New York: Atheneum, 1968.

Hrvatski vojnički koledar 1908. Agram: 1908.

Jenks, W. A. Austrian Electoral Reform of 1907. New York: Columbia University Press, 1950.

Kerner, R. J., Ed. Yugoslavia. Berkeley: University of California Press, 1949.

Larson, Gustive O. _Outline History of Territorial Utah_. 1958 rpt. Provo: Brigham Young University, 1972.

Larson, Gustive O. _Prelude to the Kingdom_. Francestown: Marshall Jones Company, 1947.

Macartney, C. A. _The Habsburg Empire 1790-1918_. New York: MacMillan Company, 1969.

Palmer, Alan. _The Lands Between: A History of East-Central Europe since the Congress of Vienna_. New York: MacMillan Company, 1970.

Prpic, George J. _The Croatian Immigrants in America_. New York: Philosophical Library, 1971.

St. Ehrlich, Vera. _Family in Transition: A Study of 300 Yugoslav Villages_. Princeton: Princeton University Press, 1966.

Seton-Watson, R. W. _The Southern Slav Question and the Hapsburg Monarchy_. 1911 rpt. New York: Howard Fertig, 1969.

Stavrianos, L. S. _The Balkans Since 1453_. New York: Holt, Rinehart, and Winston, Inc., 1966.

Stavrianos, L. S. _The Balkans 1815-1914_. New York: Holt, Rinehart, and Winston, Inc. 1963.

Stein, Maurice R. _The Eclipse of Community: An Interpretation of American Studies_. New York: Harper and Row, 1960.

Tomasevich, Jozo. _Peasants, Politics, and Economic Change in Yugoslavia_. Stanford: Stanford University Press, 1955.

Tyler, Alice Felt. _Freedom's Ferment_. 1944 rpt. New York: Harper and Row, 1962.

Vogt, Evon Z., and Albert, Ethel M. _People of Rimrock: A Study of Values in Five Cultures_. Cambridge: Harvard University Press, 1966.

Wolff, Robert Lee. _Balkans in Our Time_. New York: W. W. Norton and Company, Inc., 1967.

Zavertnik, Jože, Ed. _Ameriski Slovenci_. Chicago: Slovenske Narodne Podporne Jednote, 1925.

Articles

Austin, B. "Sidelights of the Balkan Wars." _Living Age_, 276 (February 1913), p. 259-264.

Bailey, W. F. "Life in Croatia." Edinburgh Review, 220 (October 1914), p. 362-371.

Bonsal, Stephen. "The Sons of the Eagle." North American Review, 97, No. 1 (1913), p. 124-135.

Curti, Merle and Birr, Kendall. "The Immigrant and the American Image in Europe, 1860-1914." Mississippi Valley Historical Review, 37, No. 2 (September 1950), p. 203-220.

Krizman, Bogdan. "Serbian War Mission to the U.S.A." Jugoslovenski Istorijski Casopis, 1, No. 2 (1968), p. 43-73.

Mulder, William. "Image of Zion: Mormonism as an Influence in Scandinavia." Mississippi Valley Historical Review, 43, No. 1 (June 1956), p. 18-38.

Mulder, William. "Through Immigrant Eyes: Utah History at the Grass Roots." Utah Historical Quarterly, 22, No. 1 (January 1954), p. 46.

Papanikolas, Helen Z. "Toil and Rage in a New Land: the Greek Immigrants in Utah." Utah Historical Quarterly, 38, No. 2 (Spring 1970).

Rothenberg, G. A. "The Croatian Military Border and the Rise of Yugoslav Nationalism." Slavonic and East European Review, 43, No. 100 (December 1964), p. 34-46.

Sherwood, H. F. "Those Who Go Back." Harper's Weekly (20 July 1912), p. 18

Steiner, A. "Spirit of the Balkans." Outlook, 102, No. 9 (1912), p. 534-536.

Newspapers

Bingham Press Bulletin.

Deseret News.

Eastern Utah Advocate.

Narodni Glasnik.

Prosveta.

Salt Lake Tribune.

Srbobran (American).

Documents

Declaration of Intention, U. S. Department of Labor, Naturalization Service Form 2203.

Eleventh Census of the United States. Washington, D.C.: GPO, 1890.

Fourteenth Census of the United States. Washington, D.C.: GPO, 1922.

Human Relations Area Files.

Inventory of the County Archives of Utah No. 4, Carbon County. Ogden: Utah Historical Records Survey Project, 1940.

Report of the Select Committee of the House of Representatives to Inquire into the Alleged Violation of the Laws Prohibiting the Importation of Contract Laborers, Paupers, Convicts, and Other Classes, Together With the Testimony, Documents, and Consular Reports Submitted to the Committee. Washington, D.C.: GPO, 1888.

Reports of Diplomatic and Consular Officers Concerning Emigration From Europe to the United States. Washington, D.C.: GPO, 1889

Ripley, William Z. "The European Population of the United States." Annual Report of the Board of Regents of the Smithsonian Institution Showing the Operations, Expenditures and Condition of the Institution for the Year Ending June 30, 1909. Washington, D.C.: GPO, 1910.

Thirteenth Census of the United States. Washington, D.C.: GPO, 1913.

Utah, Facts and Figures Pertaining to Utah (Second Report of the State Bureau of Immigration, Labor and Statistics). Salt Lake City: Arrow Press, 1915.

Utah, First Report of the State Bureau of Immigration, Labor and Statistics. Salt Lake City: Arrow Press, 1913.

Utah, Public Documents, Sec. 11, Coal Inspector's Report. Salt Lake City: 1903-1904.

Utah, Third District Court Cases. Salt Lake City: 1920

Interviews

The following is a list of interviews conducted by Joseph Stipanovich and recorded on magnetic tape.

Croats

George Pezell, July 1972, Salt Lake City, Utah

Tonka Bolic, August 1972, Salt Lake City, Utah

Walter Bolic, August 1972, Salt Lake City, Utah

John Dunoskovich, September 1972, Midvale, Utah

Matt Star, January 1973, Helper, Utah

Mary Zagar Dupin, December 1972, Helper, Utah

Martin Kramerich, January 1973, Helper, Utah

Zorka Bogden, September 1972, Midvale, Utah

Joseph Mazuran, December 1972, Midvale, Utah

Marko Yelinich, February 1973, Helper, Utah

Katie Star, February 1973, Helper, Utah

Caroline Tomsic, March 1973, Helper, Utah

Serbs

Joe Hinich, June 1972, Salt Lake City, Utah

Bessie Hinich, June 1972, Salt Lake City, Utah

Mike Dragos, June 1972, Salt Lake City, Utah

Millie Dragos, June 1972, Salt Lake City, Utah

Ely Sasich, June 1972, Salt Lake City, Utah

Peter Klasna, July 1972, Salt Lake City, Utah

Ely Klasna, July 1972, Salt Lake City, Utah

Pete N. Stipanovich, September 1972, Salt Lake City, Utah

Joseph Church, October 1972, Leadmine, Utah

Milka Smilanich, December 1972, Leadmine, Utah

Grey J. Melich, January 1973, Murray, Utah

Joe Mikich, January 1973, Midvale, Utah

Slovenes

Rasa Pirc, July 1972, Salt Lake City, Utah

John Skerl, January 1973, Spring Glen, Utah

Joe Chesnik, January 1973, Helper, Utah

Tony Klarich, January 1973, Price, Utah

John Cvar, January 1973, Midvale, Utah

V. Vouk, February 1973, Price, Utah

Frances Vouk, February 1973, Price, Utah

Caroline Skerl, February 1973, Helper, Utah

Rudy Rebol, February 1973, Helper, Utah

VITA

Name	Joseph Stipanovich
Birthplace	Kansas City, Kansas
Birthdate	November 27, 1946
High School	Salt Lake Evening High School
University 1967-1970	University of Utah Salt Lake City, Utah
Degree 1970	B.S., University of Utah Salt Lake City, Utah
Certificates 1970	Certificate in International Relations University of Utah Salt Lake City, Utah
Military Service 1964-1967	U. S. Army
Professional Positions	Intern, Bureau of Immigration and Naturalization, Department of Justice, Washington, D.C., 1969; Research assistant, American West Center, University of Utah, Salt Lake City, Utah, 1972-73.

INDEX

Salt Lake City, 6, 86, 91.
San Francisco, 34.
Sarajevo, 29.
Serbian Benevolent Society, 52,
   54-55.
Serb National Federation, 53, 61.
Serbs, 23-24, 28-29, 31-32, 37,
   41, 46, 54-55, 57-59, 61, 63-64,
   75, 83, 85-86, 93, 97.
Skerl, John, 65.
Slovenes, 23, 27, 31-33, 38-41,
   46, 55-57, 61, 63-66, 75, 78,
   83, 85, 90, 93, 97, 105.
Slovenian National Home (Helper),
   105-106.
Smith, Hyrum, 4.
Smith, Joseph, 4-5.
Soldier Summit, 62.
South Slavs. Also see Serbs;
   Croats; Slovenes; Bulgars;
   Macedonians. 19, 28-32,
   35-39, 41, 46-48, 50, 53,
   55-57, 60-64, 66, 71-73, 75-76,
   78-79, 81, 84, 87, 89-90,
   92-93, 97-99, 102-104, 107-109.
Spring Canyon, 63.
Srpski Narodni Savez. See Serb
   National Federation.
Standardville, 63.
Stipanovich, Ivan, 93.
Sumner, Charles, 16.
Sunnyside, 63.

T

Trieste, 103.
Trinidad, 36, 38, 100.

V

Vienna, 29.
Vojvodina, 23.

W

West Virginia, 34.
Wisconsin, 34.

Y

Young, Brigham, 5-7, 12.
Yugoslavia, 92-93.
Yugoslavs. See South
   Slavs.

Z

Zagreb, 38.
Zion, 1, 6.